WATCHDOGS, BLOGS AND WILD HOGS

A Collection of Quotations on Media

WATCHDOGS, BLOGS AND WILD HOGS

A Collection of Quotations on Media

GORDON S. JACKSON

NEW MEDIA VENTURES INC.

Spokane, Washington

Published by

NEW MEDIA VENTURES INC.

New Media Ventures, Inc.
2006

Gordon S. Jackson
Watchdogs, Blogs and Wild Hogs: A Collection of Quotations on Media
1. Reference   2. Quotations   3. Media   4. Newspapers and The Press
Includes index.

ISBN: 0-923910-24-7

I. Gordon S. Jackson

New Media Ventures, Inc., Spokane, Washington

First Edition

Design: The Oxalis Group in association with Integrated Composition Systems

Set in 12/14 Times
Paginated in Quark by Integrated Composition Systems, Spokane, Washington.

Printed and bound by Thomson-Shore, Dexter, Michigan
on Glatfelter 60# Natures Natural Paper, which is acid-free
and 90 percent recycled from at least 50 percent post-consumer
waste. It meets the minimum requirements of American National
Standard for Information Sciences—Permanence of Paper for
Printed Library Materials, ANSI Z39.48–1984.♾♲

For Ed Lambeth—
a model journalist, scholar,
mentor and friend

Contents

Acknowledgments — vii

Introduction — ix

The Quotations — 1

  Advertising — 3

  Books — 11

  Broadcasting — 18

  The Business of Media — 20

  Censorship — 26

  Columnists — 35

  Credibility, Accuracy and Bias — 39

  Critics and Reviewers — 43

  Democracy and the Media — 46

  Editorials — 49

  Editors and Editing — 51

  Ethics, Values and Standards — 56

  The First Amendment — 62

  Freedom of Expression — 66

  Freelance — 78

  Government and the Media — 80

  The Internet — 84

  Journalism — 90

  Journalists — 100

  Language and Words — 105

Law 110
Magazines 114
Miscellaneous 117
Mottos and Slogans 125
Movies 127
News 133
Newspapers 142
Photojournalism and Photographers 152
Politics, Politicians and the Media 157
Power and Influence 162
Presidents, the Presidency and the Media 165
The Press 170
Print and Printing 174
Propaganda 177
The Public and Public Opinion 181
Public Relations 183
Radio 188
Readers and Reading 192
Recording Industry 195
Reporters and Reporting 199
Sources and Subjects 204
Sports 211
Tabloids 213
Technology and the Media 215
Television 220
Television News 234
War and the Media 240
Writers and Writing 245

Index of Names 255

Acknowledgments

The following individuals played an important part in bringing this anthology to completion. Gail Fielding in Whitworth College's library helped to procure material via inter-library loan. My thanks are due to Martha Brown, my erstwhile assistant at Whitworth, and my daughter, Sarah Jackson, who helped in preparing the manuscript. Sarah also embodied the virtues of the editor's role described in this volume, by catching numerous errors in the manuscript and offering helpful suggestions for refining the selection of quotations. My son, Matthew Jackson, brought his uncanny gift for catching typos to the final proofreading stage. K. G. Kim was helpful in providing an international dimension to this collection.

My colleagues in the Whitworth College Communications Department, Jim McPherson and Ginny Whitehouse, were generous in letting me raid their libraries. In addition, Jim offered valuable comments that helped shape the final draft of the manuscript.

Nora Lessersohn did a superb job copy editing the manuscript. By constantly asking, "Are you sure this is right?" she helped me catch error after error and identified those places where a brief clarification would strengthen either the quote itself or the attribution. Thanks are due also to Julie Read of New Media Ventures, who did the final manuscript preparation, and to Steve Smith, editor of *The Spokesman-Review*, who saw a potential match between this anthology and NMV, and steered me toward NMV's publisher and editor-in-chief Shaun O.L. Higgins. And it is to Shaun whom I owe the largest thank you, for his enthusiastic readiness to take on this project and for his encouragement at each step in bringing the book to completion.

Introduction

Americans have a peculiar love-hate relationship with their media. On the one hand, much of the public seems to regard the media's watchdog role, of gathering and reporting information, with skepticism, cynicism or outright disdain. While they may still believe this surveillance function is essential in a democratic society—and even this premise appears to be losing support—these Americans have growing doubts about their media's ability to fill this role. One survey after another shows that many Americans view their news coverage today as biased, intrusive, sensationalized, often inaccurate, and generally lacking in credibility.

On the other hand, the public's love affair with the media's entertainment offerings is probably more passionate than ever, especially for those under 40. (Think iPod or MTV.) Those of us who teach traditional-age college students about the media need only to put them on a 24-hour media fast to see the grip that music, in particular, has on this generation. Perceptive media critics, like the late Neil Postman, have noted how "the rhetoric of entertainment" has increasingly come to shape all aspects of our culture—whether it's the evening news or even a church service on Sunday morning. Hence the title of Postman's book, *Are We Amusing Ourselves to Death?*

The two most recent U.S. presidential elections reflect what could be a deepening ideological, cultural and political divide in the United States. Not surprisingly, this divide is reflected in how voters view the media. Many on the political right, and even in the center, see the "mainstream media" as dominated by a left-of-center view of things that is out of touch with mainstream American values, and whose news coverage is therefore to be viewed with suspicion, or perhaps even total skepticism. Those on the left side of the ideological spectrum may agree that there is bias, but they see it through quite different lenses. In addition, they also are deeply troubled by the growing concentration of media power as fewer and fewer corporate conglomerates dominate the media. As we move toward media oligopoly, they ask, how can we trust a watchdog that increasingly barks only with its master's voice?

Large sectors of the population thus question the media's ability or commitment to act as independent monitors of government, business, the courts and other major institutions. Several episodes over the past decade have soured the public's attitude toward this traditional watchdog role, including coverage of the O. J. Simpson trial, the discredited memo about President Bush's National Guard Service which Dan Rather reported during the 2004 presidential election, and Jayson Blair's fabrications in *The New York Times*. Reaching back a little further, the Janet Cooke episode required *The Washington Post* to return a Pulitzer Prize won for stunning—but, it turned out, false—reporting.

Those in the media who continue to take this watchdog role seriously face pressures beyond this skepticism from many whom they seek to serve. One pressure is the ever-present tension between serving the public interest (by providing news) and generating the profits needed to stay in business and satisfy shareholders and other owners. There is also the need to come to terms with new technology, such as the role of bloggers and how they and Internet technology are already changing the way people send and receive news.

Another factor, noted above, is American society's insatiable demand for entertainment. How will this shape the content of our movies or talk radio? How will we pay for our personal, and potentially highly personalized, music in 10 years time? And what will become of our local newspaper and local TV news? Will almost everything gravitate more and more toward tabloid treatment of the news, because that is where the profits lie? In other words, will media providers offer matters of substance, with the day's equivalent of live televised hearings on the Vietnam War? See for example Fred Friendly's quote on why he resigned as head of CBS news when his network would not cover this event. Or, will we consumers ultimately prefer a news diet dominated by tabloid tales like *A Wild Hog Ate My Baby* (the title of a history of tabloid journalism)?

As many of this anthology's quotes say in one way or another, the U.S. media face fundamental questions about their present role and how this role will change tomorrow. It seems all agree about one thing, however: the power and potential influence of the media in contemporary society. Nicholas Johnson has said of the United States, "We may already have reached the point in this country where the media, our greatest check on other accumulations of power, may themselves be beyond the reach of any other institutions." Whether or not one agrees with Johnson, a former Federal Communications Commissioner, there is no disputing the massive influence the media have in all spheres of contemporary U.S. life. His comment applies equally to many other countries, too, as the mass media have shaped lives around the world to a degree unimaginable only a century ago.

A rich array of responses has accompanied the media's rise to worldwide prominence, as media insiders and observers have reflected on this institution's character, role and performance. This anthology provides a sampling of these responses and seeks to offer a unique array of quotations on all the major media and a selection of related topics. This collection thus offers insights on the media as a whole, unlike more specialized collections of quotations on single topics like freedom of expression or the film industry.

This anthology is intended to meet three objectives. One is to help anyone wanting to find a specific quotation—to check the wording, the source, or both. ("Just what *did* Spiro Agnew say when calling media leaders "nattering nabobs of negativism"?) Another is to provide a variety of insights on a particular aspect of the media, to provoke thought, or to offer quotes to enliven a news story, research paper, or speech. A third objective is simply to offer the pleasure of browsing through observations, reflections, insults and predictions on nearly fifty related topics, ranging from "Advertising" to "Writers and Writing."

However you use this collection, you will recognize some quotes instantly, like "All the News That's Fit to Print," the slogan of *The New York Times*; the wording of the First Amendment to the U.S. Constitution; or Marshall McLuhan's, "The medium is the message." Others will be unfamiliar. All have been selected to meet one criterion: does this quote in some way add to our understanding of the mass media that surround us, or express what others think about them. A quote may have historical significance, or offer particular wisdom in understanding one of the media. Or perhaps it provides a funny, ironic, or provocative viewpoint, like the statement that the human race is faced with the cruel choice "of work or daytime television," or the claim in the silent movie era by Harry Warner of Warner Brothers studios, "Who the hell wants to hear actors talk?"

The sources of the quotes are as wide-ranging as their tone. Many are from media practitioners, including pioneers in advertising, movies, newspapering, public relations, radio and television. Others are from informal observers or critics of the media, including presidents, celebrities or ordinary mortals on the receiving end of media attention. Yet others are from academics, whose business it is to study the media and their role in society. My objective in selecting the topics was to keep the focus on the media themselves, and to reflect a mix of areas that proved to be the most "quote-rich," as well as my own interests. The quotes are drawn overwhelmingly from the United States and other Western nations. This is both because these countries provide a great preponderance of quotes in English, and because this is where the mass media have the longest history.

I have kept notes and explanations to a minimum. Dates,

identifications and other information are provided only when I have thought they are helpful in appreciating the quote or its context more fully. Several quotes surface in various forms or have more than one author to whom the quote is attributed; in those cases where original wording or authorship was impossible to verify, the most authoritative version or author is cited. To assure accuracy, the many quotes that use male-dominant language are left unchanged.

This anthology is drawn from my personal collection of quotations compiled during my years as a journalist, graduate student of the media, and journalism professor, and from other general and media-specific anthologies. I am also deeply indebted to the scores of books on the media on which I have relied. Virtually all the quotes are from print sources; only a handful are drawn from the Internet. Among the most helpful resources I found were:

American Newspaper Publishers Association Foundation: *Speaking of a Free Press*
Robert Andrews: *The Concise Columbia Dictionary of Quotations*
Stephen Bates: *If No News, Send Rumors*
Donald Brandt: *Freedom is First: A Selection of Quotations on the Values of Free Expression*
Ralph Emerson Browns: *The New Dictionary of Thoughts*
Wesley D. Camp: *Camp's Unfamiliar Quotations from 2000 BC to the Present*
Gorton Carruth and Eugene Ehrlich: *American Quotations*
J. M. and M. J. Cohen: *The Penguin Dictionary of Modern Quotations*
J. M. and M. J. Cohen: *The Penguin Dictionary of Quotations*
Collins Quotation Finder
Paul Dickson: *The Official Rules*
Lewis D. Eigen and Jonathan P. Siegel: *The Macmillan Dictionary of Political Quotations*
Bergen Evans: *Dictionary of Quotations*

Robert I. Fitzhenry: *The Fitzhenry and Whiteside Book of Quotations*

The Freedom Forum—miscellaneous resources

Elizabeth Frost-Knappman: *The World Almanac of Presidential Quotations*

Jenny Hobbs: *Paper Prophets*

Percival E. Jackson: *Wisdom of the Supreme Court*

Gordon S. Jackson: *Never Scratch a Tiger with a Short Stick*

Gordon S. Jackson: *Outside Insights*

Alison Jones: *Chambers Dictionary of Quotations*

Elizabeth Knowles: *The Oxford Dictionary of Modern Quotations*

Robert A. Nowlan and Gwendolyn Nowlan: *A Dictionary of Quotations about Communication*

The Oxford Dictionary of Quotations (3rd ed.)

Alan Warwick Palmer: *Quotations in History*

Matthew Parris and Phil Mason: *Read My Lips*

Christopher Paul and James J. Kim: *Reporters on the Battlefield*

Laurence Peter: *Peter's Quotations*

Kathryn Petras and Ross Petras: *The Whole World Book of Quotations*

Keen Rafferty: *That's What They Said About The Press*

Connie Robertson: *The Wordsworth Dictionary of Quotations*

James B. Simpson: *Simpson's Contemporary Quotations*
Who Said What

While great care has been taken to ensure the accuracy and authenticity of each quote, inaccuracies have no doubt crept into this collection. I will correct any errors that are brought to my attention in any future editions of this volume.

Gordon S. Jackson

WATCHDOGS, BLOGS AND WILD HOGS

A Collection of Quotations on Media

Advertising

Advertising makes you think you've wanted something all your life that you've never heard of before.

—Anonymous

When the client moans and sighs
Make his logo twice the size.
If he should still prove refractory,
Show a picture of his factory.
Only in the gravest cases
Should you show the clients' faces.

—Anonymous jingle quoted by David Ogilvy

Good times, bad times, there will always be advertising. In good times, people want to advertise; in bad times they have to.

—Bruce Barton

The immense nausea of advertisements.

—Charles Baudelaire

The advertisements in a newspaper are more full of knowledge in respect to what is going on in a state or community than the editorial columns are.

—Henry Ward Beecher

If it's news, no amount of advertising will keep it out of the paper; if it isn't news, no amount of advertising will get it in.

—Creed Black, newspaper publisher

Advertisements as a whole may be completely misleading although every sentence separately considered is literally true.

—*Hugo Black*

The deeper problems connected with advertising come less from the unscrupulousness of our "deceivers" than from our pleasure in being deceived; less from the desire to seduce than from the desire to be seduced.

—*Daniel J. Boorstin*

Doing business without advertising is like winking at a girl in the dark. You know what you are doing, but nobody else does.

—*Steuart Henderson Britt*

From any cross-section of ads, the general advertiser's attitude would seem to be: if you are a lousy, smelly, idle, underprivileged and over-sexed status-seeking neurotic moron, give me your money.

—*Kenneth Bromfield*

Sanely applied advertising could remake the world.

—*Stuart Chase*

Advertising is what you do when you can't go to see somebody. That's all it is.

—*Fairfax Cone*

Most of the viewers who fear [TV] advertising as an evil force give it too much credit. About all it can do . . . is to exploit a given interest, predilection, disposition, prejudice or bias and bring this to bear on a buying decision.

—*Fairfax Cone*

To be effective, advertising must relate to society as it is, not to society as we think it should be. Blaming advertising for the ills of society is like blaming your mirror for the wart on your nose.

—*Draper Daniels*

Advertising

You can tell the ideals of a nation by its advertisements.

—Norman Douglas

As to the idea that advertising motivates people, remember the Edsel.

—Peter Drucker

He [British radio commentator John Snagge] had been against commercial broadcasting ever since he heard a Toscanini radio concert in New York interrupted by the sponsor's slogan "It may be December outside, ladies; but it is always August under your armpits."

—Evening Standard *(London)*

The philosophy behind much advertising is based on the old observation that every man is really two men—the man he is and the man he wants to be.

—William Feather

Advertising deals in open sores. . . . Fear. Greed. Anger. Hostility. You name the dwarfs and we play on every one. We play on all the emotions and on all the problems, from not getting ahead . . . to the desire to be one of the crowd. Everyone has a button. If enough people have the same button, you have a successful ad and a successful product.

—Jerry Della Femina

Advertising is the most fun you can have with your clothes on.

—Jerry Della Femina

[Advertising's] contribution to humanity is exactly minus zero.

—F. Scott Fitzgerald

We grew up founding our dreams on the infinite promise of American advertising. I still believe that one can learn to play

5

the piano by mail and that mud will give you a perfect complexion.

—Zelda Fitzgerald

The advertising man is a liaison between the products of business and the mind of the nation. He must know both before he can serve either.

—Glenn Frank

Few people at the beginning of the nineteenth century needed an adman to tell them what they wanted.

—John Kenneth Galbraith

No space today is safe. Ads are placed on the backs of airplane seats, at eyeball height over urinals, on the backs of stall doors in women's bathrooms. In 2000, ABC installed motion-sensitive talking ads in a thousand public urinals in New York and Los Angeles to promote a new sitcom.

—Todd Gitlin

The guy you've really got to reach with your advertising is the copywriter for your chief rival's advertising agency. If you can terrorize him, you've got it licked.

—Howard L. Gossage

Commercial advertising might well be called the stepchild of the First Amendment. . . . [Yet] advertising is a medium of information and persuasion, providing much of the day-to-day "education" of the American public and facilitating the flexible allocation of resources necessary to a free enterprise economy. Neither profit motivation nor desire to influence private economic decisions necessarily distinguishes the peddler from the preacher, the publisher or the politician.

—Harvard Business Review

Advertisement is one of the most interesting and difficult of modern literary forms.

—Aldous Huxley

Advertisements contain the only truths to be relied on in a newspaper.

—Thomas Jefferson

Advertisements are now so numerous that they are very negligently perused, and it is therefore become necessary to gain attention by magnificence of promises, and by eloquences sometimes sublime and sometimes pathetic.

—Samuel Johnson, 1709–1784

The trade of advertising is now so near perfection that it is not easy to propose any advancement.

—Samuel Johnson

Advertising is the lubricant for the free-enterprise system.

—Leo-Arthur Kelmenson

Advertising people use great music, they take lines of great poetry and distort them—if they could get away with it, they would use the crucifixion to advertise nails.

—Robert Kirby

Advertising may be defined as the art of arresting human intelligence long enough to get money from it.

—Stephen Leacock

Advertising is a valuable economic factor because it is the cheapest way of selling goods, particularly if the goods are worthless.

—Sinclair Lewis

The best ad is a good product.

—Alan H. Meyer

Advertising is the garment of abundance.

—*Marshall McLuhan*

Advertising is the greatest art form of the twentieth century.

—*Marshall McLuhan*

And let us remind readers regularly, in editorials, in our promotional advertising, in speeches to civic groups and others, that advertising helps people live better and saves them money.

—*Paul Miller, CEO of Gannett*

I think that I shall never see
A billboard lovely as a tree
Indeed unless the billboards falls
I'll never see a tree at all.

—*Ogden Nash*

It isn't advertising *anything*, dammit.
   —*Father to a small boy looking at a rainbow, in a* New Yorker *cartoon*

The consumer is not a moron. She is your wife.

—*David Ogilvy*

Ninety-nine percent of advertising doesn't sell much of anything.

—*David Ogilvy*

Advertising is the rattling of a stick inside a swill bucket.

—*George Orwell*

The true role of advertising is exactly that of the first salesman hired by the first manufacturer—to get business away from his competitors.

—*Rosser Reeves*

Advertising

It is very difficult to have a free, fair and honest press anywhere in the world. . . . As a rule, papers are largely supported by advertising, and that immediately gives the advertisers a certain hold over the medium which they use.

—*Eleanor Roosevelt*

If I were starting life over again, I am inclined to think that I would go into the advertising business in preference to almost any other. The general raising of the standards of modern civilization among all groups of people during the past half-century would have been impossible without the spreading of the knowledge of higher standards by means of advertising.

—*Franklin D. Roosevelt*

Advertising is the modern substitute for argument; its function is to make the worse appear the better.

—*George Santayana*

With no ads, who would pay for the media? The good fairy?

—*Samuel Thurm, of the Association of National Advertisers*

Advertising can't sell any product; it can only help to sell a product the people want to buy.

—*Jeremy Tunstall*

Advertising is the whip which hustles humanity up the road to the Better Mousetrap. It is the vision which reproaches man for the paucity of his desires.

—*E. S. Turner*

Advertising has annihilated the power of the most powerful adjectives.

—*Paul Valéry*

Half the money I spend on advertising is wasted, and the trouble is I don't know which half.

—John Wanamaker, paraphrasing Lord Leverhulme

Advertising is the genie which is transforming America into a place of comfort, luxury and ease for millions.

—William Allen White

See also *Propaganda; Public Relations*

Books

A book is a success when people who haven't read it pretend they have.

—*Anonymous*

The reason why so few good books are written is that so few people who can write know anything.

—*Walter Bagehot*

Without books God is silent.

—*Thomas Bartholin*

When I am dead, I hope it may be said:
"His sins were scarlet, but his books were read."

—*Hilaire Belloc*

Books are the compasses and telescopes and sextants and charts which other men have prepared to help us navigate the dangerous seas of human life.

—*Jesse Lee Bennett*

A best seller was a book which somehow sold well simply because it was selling well.

—*Daniel J. Boorstin*

I have always imagined that Paradise will be a kind of library.

—*Jorge Luis Borges*

My books are friends that never fail me.

—Thomas Carlyle

"What is the use of a book," thought Alice, "without pictures and conversation?"

—Lewis Carroll

It is chiefly through books that we enjoy intercourse with superior minds. In the best books, great men talk to us, give us their most precious thoughts, and pour their souls into ours. God be thanked for books. They are the voices of the distant and the dead, and make us heirs of the spiritual life of past ages.

—William Ellery Channing

You cannot open a book without learning something.

—Chinese proverb

As repressed sadists are supposed to become policemen or butchers so those with an irrational fear of life become publishers.

—Cyril Connolly

The wise are above books.

—Samuel Daniel

The reading of all good books is like conversation with the finest men of past centuries.

—René Descartes

Never judge a book by its movie.

—J. W. Eagan

Every book must be chewed to get out its juice.

—English proverb

Books

When I get a little money, I buy books; and if any is left, I buy food and clothes.

—*Erasmus*

Books can be dangerous. The best ones should be labeled: This could change your life.

—*Helen Exley*

Never lend books, for no one ever returns them; the only books I have in my library are books that other folk have lent me.

—*Anatole France*

The canny of the publishers know that an enormous popular appetite for the insulting of the famous must be gratified, and the modern biographer emerges from the editorial conference a sadist and a wiser man.

—*Florence Kipper Frank*

Even bad books are books and therefore sacred.

—*Günter Grass*

Thank you for sending me a copy of your book. I'll waste no time reading it.

—*Moses Hadas*

Books give not wisdom where none was before.
But where some is, there reading makes it more.

—*John Harrington*

If you would understand your own age, read the works of fiction produced in it. People in disguise speak freely.

—*Arthur Helps*

Read for ideas, not for authors.

—*Oliver Wendell Holmes Jr.*

Make books thy companions. Let thy cases and shelves be thy pleasure grounds and gardens.

—Judah ibn-Tibbon

There is no worse robber than a bad book.

—Italian proverb

If you drop gold and books, pick up the books first, then the gold.

—Jewish proverb

A book must be an ice axe to break the frozen sea within us.

—Franz Kafka

Everywhere I have sought rest and not found it, except sitting in a corner by myself with a little book.

—Thomas à Kempis

The novel's spirit is the spirit of complexity. Every novel says to the reader, "Things are not as simple as you think."

—Milan Kundera

Those who refuse to lend their books . . . shall be fined.

—Latvian Jewish Community Council, 1736

It certainly is my opinion that a book worth reading only in childhood is not worth reading even then.

—C. S. Lewis

Books are like mirrors; if a monkey peeps into one you can't expect an angel to be reflected.

—Georg Christoph Lichtenberg

The multitude of books is a great evil. There is no measure or limit to this fever of writing; everyone must be an author;

some out of vanity to acquire celebrity; others for the sake of lucre and gain.

—*Martin Luther*

A person who publishes a book appears willfully in public with his pants down.

—*Edna St. Vincent Millay*

A book is the only place in which you can examine a fragile thought without breaking it, or explore an explosive idea without fear it will go off in your face. It is one of the few havens remaining where a man's mind can get both provocation and privacy.

—*Edward P. Morgan*

The real purpose of books is to trap the mind into doing its own thinking.

—*Christopher Morley*

A dose of poison can do its work only once, but a bad book can go on poisoning people's minds for any length of time.

—*John Murray*

Whoever is able to write a book and does not, is as if he has lost a child.

—*Nachman of Bratslav*

All books are divisible into two classes, the books of the hour and the books of all time.

—*John Ruskin*

Buying books would be a good thing if one could also buy the time to read them in: but as a rule the purchase of books is mistaken for the appropriation of their contents.

—*Arthur Schopenhauer*

Today the publishing marketplace is dominated by Hollywood, by the agents, and by the sale of subsidiary rights. . . . To my grandfather the book business today would be unrecognizable. It belongs to the entertainment industry much more than to the literary world.

—Charles Scribner

The profession of book-writing makes horse racing seem like a solid, stable business.

—John Steinbeck

Books are good enough in their own way, but they are a mighty bloodless substitute for life.

—Robert Louis Stevenson

To read too many books is harmful.

—Mao Tse-Tung

Books are the carriers of civilization. Without books, history is silent, literature dumb, science crippled, thought and speculation at a standstill.

—Barbara Tuchman

A good book is the best of friends, the same today and for ever.

—Martin Tupper

A classic is something that everybody wants to have read and nobody wants to read.

—Mark Twain

The man who doesn't read good books has no advantage over the man who can't read them.

—Mark Twain

When I was in prison I was wrapped up in all those deep books. That Tolstoy crap. People shouldn't read that stuff.

—Mike Tyson

We have a natural right to make use of our pens as of our tongue, at our peril, risk, and hazard. I know many books which have bored their readers, but I know of none which has done real evil.

—Voltaire

It is with books as with men—a very small number play a great part; the rest are lost in the multitude.

—Voltaire

The multitude of books is making us ignorant.

—Voltaire (attributed)

Beware you be not swallowed up in books! An ounce of love is worth a pound of knowledge.

—John Wesley

There is no such thing as a moral or an immoral book. Books are well written or badly written.

—Oscar Wilde

See also *Writing*

Broadcasting

Television just feeds you. Radio involves you.

—Himan Brown

The proliferation of radio and television channels has produced a wilderness of cave-dwellers instead of the promised global village.

—Phillip Howard

[W]e had to learn what our new broadcasting medium was for. Some people thought broadcasting would be for education. Some thought merely that it would replace the phonograph. Some thought it would remake the world, which it hasn't. Some thought it would revolutionize politics, which it has. . . . But, of course, broadcasting did not limit itself to any one of these. Instead, it became almost all the things that were imagined for it.

—William S. Paley, 1954

If any licensee shall permit any person who is a legally qualified candidate for any public office to use a broadcasting station, he shall afford equal opportunities to all other such candidates for that office in the use of such broadcasting station . . .

—Radio Act of 1927

Radio and television, to which we devote so many of the leisure hours once spent listening to parlor chatter and parlor music, have succeeded in lifting the manufacture of banality out of the sphere of handicraft and placed it in that of a major industry.

—Nathalie Sarraute

There was once a wicked lady called Circe, who was reputed to turn human beings into swine. The object of broadcasting should be the exact opposite.

—James Shelley

Television contracts the imagination and radio expands it.

—Terry Wogan

See also *Radio, Television, TV News*

The Business of Media

Our constitutional theory is in the grip of a romantic conception of free expression, a belief that the "marketplace of ideas" is freely accessible. But if ever there were a self operating marketplace of ideas, it has long ceased to exist. . . . There is inequality in the power to communicate ideas just as there is inequality in economic bargaining power; to recognize the latter and deny the former is quixotic.

—*Jerome Barron*

We newspapers are very big on profits these days. We're a business, just like any other business, except that we employ English majors.

—*Dave Barry*

The commercial press is not a free press, and it is not a public service organization. It is business, big business, and as such is motivated by one principle—profit.

—*Jules E. Bernfeld*

The market will pay better to entertain than educate.

—*Warren Buffet*

In the final analysis the only Achilles heel in our present-day newspapers is that they are large capitalistic enterprises. As such, some of them, when their own selfish interests are involved, are in greater or lesser degree, dishonest.

—*John Cowles*

The American press, with a very few exceptions, is a kept press. Kept by big corporations the way a whore is kept by a rich man.

—Theodore Dreiser

We have no obligation to make history. We have no obligation to make art. We have no obligation to make a statement. To make money is our only obligation.

—Michael Eisner, Disney CEO

Today's [media] deals may weigh on the culture for decades.

—Todd Gitlin

While the number of TV channels and media outlets is burgeoning, ownership and control of our mainstream media, both print and electronic, are becoming increasingly concentrated.... Today, a few conglomerates, which have no direct responsibility to the American public, wield extraordinary power over the ideas and the information the public can receive.

—Lawrence K. Grossman, 1991

It is clear that the press is itself in a sort of dilemma; it can cease neither to be big business nor to judge big business. From this point of view, the stock complaint that the American press voices a dominantly "capitalist" outlook is less a criticism than a truism.

—William Ernest Hocking

Television is the business of gathering you and selling you like cattle to the advertisers.

—Nicholas Johnson

Manners maketh the man but they do not, alas, make for mass circulations.

—Paul Johnson

Dependent upon advertisers, who are themselves a part of Big Business, the newspaper owners must work within a framework which the advertisers largely define. The real guardian of their interests in the paper is then shifted from the editorial to the business side; and the stages are presently reached when the news columns of the journal differ from the advertisement columns only in that they have a different commodity to sell.

—*Harold J. Laski*

The capitalist press is the worst enemy of the people. . . . It holds the publisher's capital the most sacred thing in the world.

—*Ferdinand Lassalle*

Monopolies are like babies: nobody likes them until they have got one of their own.

—*Lord Mancroft*

The criticism that matters to [journalists] is the criticism that is implied by a reader's refusal to buy their newspaper. The marketplace dictates journalistic standards.

—*Marion Tuttle Marzolf*

By 1990, publishers of mass circulation daily newspapers will finally stop kidding themselves that they are in the newspaper business and admit that they are primarily in the business of carrying advertising messages.

—*A. Roy Megary*

Although radio broadcasting, like the press, is generally conducted on a commercial basis, it is not an ordinary business activity.

—*Frank Murphy*

I can find nothing in the Bill of Rights or the Communications Act, which says that the networks must increase their net profits each year lest the Republic collapse.

—*Edward R. Murrow*

Most media companies will find a way to stay in business. The question is whether they will find a way to stay in journalism.
—*Adam Clayton Powell III*

Once let the public come to regard the press as exclusively a commercial business, and there is an end to its moral power.
—*Joseph Pulitzer*

If you don't make a profit, you're out of business. But which business is it—journalism or show business?
—*Frank Rich*

The newspaper is of necessity something of a monopoly, and its first duty is to shun the temptations of monopoly. Its primary office is the gathering of news.
—*C. P. Scott*

Dealing with network executives is like being nibbled to death by ducks.
—*Eric Sevareid*

The bigger the information media, the less courage and freedom they allow. Bigness means weakness.
—*Eric Sevareid*

The important thing about the so-called "communications industry" is that it is basically concerned with merchandising. News is a kind of by-product and if you want to sell things, you don't want to offend anybody.
—*I. F. Stone*

Our danger is that the virtual monopolization of the media of mass expression by big capital will distort and finally abort the democratic process.
—*Evelyn John Strachey*

Freedom of the press in Britain is freedom to print such of the proprietor's prejudices as the advertisers don't object to.

—Hannen Swaffer (attributed)

I buy newspapers to make money to buy more newspapers to make more money. As for editorial content, that's the stuff you separate ads with.

—Lord Thomson (attributed)

I think that a lot of owners of newspapers get bedazzled with the importance which they think they have in the national scene and they devote more thought to editorials or some other facet of the business, whereas I am cold-bloodedly a businessman.

—Lord Thomson

I can tell you how to make money in newspapers—own them.

—Lord Thomson

We're going to end up with four or five mega-companies that control just about everything we see.

—Ted Turner

A newspaper is a private enterprise, owing nothing to the public, which grants it no franchise. It is therefore affected with no public interest. It is emphatically the product of its owner, who is selling a manufactured product at his own risk.

—Wall Street Journal *editorial, January 20, 1925*

Frank Munsey, the great publisher, is dead. Frank Munsey contributed to the journalism of his day the talent of a meat packer, the morals of a money changer, and the manners of an undertaker. He and his kind have about succeeded in transforming a once-noble profession into an 8 percent security. May he rest in trust.

—William Allen White

The people have a keen and accurate sense that much of the editorial anxiety about freedom of the press rises out of editorial greed.

—William Allen White

Every newspaper, no matter how tight the news hole, has room for a story on another newspaper increasing its newsstand price.

—Ed Zellar

See also *Advertising*

Censorship

Censorship, like poison gas, can be highly effective when the wind is blowing the right way. But the wind has a way of shifting, and sooner or later, it blows back upon the user. Whether it comes in a box or is accessed online, in the hands of the government, blocking software is toxic to a democratic society.

—American Civil Liberties Union

It is the business of a censor to acquaint us with views we didn't know we had.

—Anonymous

Obscenity is whatever gives a judge an erection.

—Anonymous

Someone has described a censor as a man who knows more than he thinks other people ought to know.

Anonymous

She flays with indignation haughty
The passages she thinks are naughty,
But reads them *carefully* so that
She'll know what to be angry at.

—Edward Anthony

And since we do not allow improper language, clearly we should also banish pictures or speeches from the stage which are indecent.

—Aristotle

By placing discretion in the hands of an official to grant or deny a license, such a statute creates a threat of censorship that by its very existence chills free speech.

—*Harry A. Blackmun*

Censorship is the younger of two ugly sisters; the name of the older is Inquisition.

—*Ludwig Börne*

It is usually better to permit a piece of trash than to suppress a work of art.

—*A. Alan Borovoy*

Those expressions are omitted which can not with propriety be read aloud in the family.

—*Thomas Bowdler, English editor and expurgator*

This film is apparently meaningless, but if it has any meaning it is doubtless objectionable.

—*British Board of Film Censors, banning Jean Cocteau's film "The Seashells and the Clergyman," 1956*

In some respects, the life of a censor is more exhilarating than that of an emperor. The best the emperor can do is snip off the heads of men and women, who are mere mortals. The censor can decapitate ideas which but for him might have lived forever.

—*Heywood Broun*

Rulers do not require the total suppression of news; it's sufficient to delay the news until it no longer matters.

—*Mark Cook and Jeff Cohen*

Let it be clear: censorship is cowardice. . . . It masks corruption. It is a school of torture: it teaches, and accustoms one to the use of force against an idea, to submit thought to an alien "other." But worse still, censorship destroys criticism, which is the essential ingredient of culture.

—*Pablo Antonio Cuadra*

God never made a man who was wise enough to be a censor.

—*Josephus Daniels*

I do not see any solution to film censorship other than its abolition.

—*Kirk Douglas*

Censorship has had a long history in the western world. Book banning is as old as books.

—*William O. Douglas*

In this nation every writer, actor, or producer, no matter what medium or expression he may use, should be freed from the censor.

—*William O. Douglas*

Censorship is like an appendix. When inert, it is useless; when active it is extremely dangerous.

—*Maurice Edelman*

Don't join the book burners. Don't think you are going to conceal faults by concealing evidence that they ever existed.

—*Dwight D. Eisenhower*

Every burned book enlightens the world.

—*Ralph Waldo Emerson*

If you open the door to censorship just a little, it never stays open just a little, and the draft that follows is always more than chilling.

—*Milos Forman*

. . . if all printers were determin'd not to print any thing till they were sure it would offend no body, there would be very little printed.

—*Benjamin Franklin*

What progress we are making. In the Middle Ages they would have burned me. Now they are content with burning my books.

—*Sigmund Freud*

When there are no papers, there is no agitation. That is why we imposed censorship.

—*Indira Gandhi*

Obscenity and hate speech alike only *become* free speech issues when their foes turn from censure to censorship. When pluralism decided to let a thousand flowers bloom, we always knew that some of them would be weeds.

—*Henry Louis Gates Jr.*

Censorship is never over for those who have experienced it. It is a brand on the imagination that affects the individual who has suffered it, forever.

—*Nadine Gordimer*

Would you allow your wife or your servant to read this book?
—*Mervyn Griffith-Jones, British lawyer during the obscenity trial on banning* Lady Chatterley's Lover

Books won't stay banned. They won't burn. Ideas won't go to jail. In the long run of history, the censor and the inquisitor have always lost. The only sure weapon against bad ideas is better ideas.

—*A. Whitney Griswold*

So many new ideas are at first strange and horrible though ultimately valuable that a very heavy responsibility rests upon those who would prevent their dissemination.

—*J. B. S. Haldane*

Wherever they burn books, they will also, in the end, burn human beings.

—*Heinrich Heine*

To limit the press is to insult a nation; to prohibit reading of certain books is to declare the inhabitants to be either fools or slaves.

—*Claude-Adrien Helvétius*

The organization of our press has truly been a success. Our law concerning the press is such that divergencies of opinion between members of the government are no longer an occasion for public exhibitions, which are not the newspapers' business. We've eliminated that conception of political freedom which holds that everybody has the right to say whatever comes into his head.

—*Adolf Hitler*

The remedy against pornography is in the hands of everyone who chooses to use it. If you do not like a book, all you have to do is not read it. Let every man be his own censor.

—*Aldous Huxley*

Did you ever hear anyone say, "That work had better be banned because I might read it and it might be very damaging to me"?

—*Joseph Henry Jackson*

Every society has a right to preserve public peace and order, and therefore has a good right to prohibit the propagation of opinions which have a dangerous tendency. . . . No member of a society has a right to teach any doctrine contrary to what the society holds to be true.

—Samuel Johnson

If nothing may be published but what civil authority shall have previously approved, power must always be the standard of truth.

—Samuel Johnson

Essentially an art of the hypocrite, censorship offers unlimited scope for the politician.

—Robert Kirby

The burning of an author's books, imprisonment for opinion's sake, has always been the tribute that an ignorant age pays to the genius of its time.

—Joseph Lewis

Why have you come into my show, austere Cato? Pray, did you walk in merely for the purpose of walking out?

—Martial

For people in power, the urge to censor is at least as strong as the sex drive.

—Larry Martz

There is one question as important—or even more important—than where we draw the line on what others can say, and that is, "Who gets to draw that line?"

—Paul McMasters

We can never be sure that the opinion we are endeavoring to stifle is a false opinion; and if we were sure, stifling it would be an evil still.

—John Stuart Mill

Censorship is nothing more than a legal corollary of public modesty.

—*Jonathan Miller*

As good almost kill a Man as kill a good Book; who kills a Man kills a reasonable creature, God's image; but hee who destroyes a good Booke, kills reason it selfe, kills the image of God, as it were in the eye. Many a man lives a burden to the Earth; but a good Booke is the pretious life-blood of a master-spirit, imbalm'd and treasur'd up on purpose to a life beyond life.

—*John Milton*

If we think to regulate printing, thereby to rectify manners, we must regulate all recreations and pastimes, all that is delightful to man.

—*John Milton*

I suppose that writers should, in a way, feel flattered by the censorship laws. They show a primitive fear and dread at the fearful magic of print.

—*John Mortimer*

The consequences of censorship are always perverse.

—*Ken Owen*

The first thing will be to establish censorship of fiction. Let the censors accept any tale that is good, and reject any that is bad.

—*Plato*

Give me six lines written by the most honorable of men, and I will find an excuse in them to hang him.

—*Cardinal Richelieu*

If in other lands the press and books and literature of all kinds are censored, we must redouble our efforts here to keep them free.

—Franklin D. Roosevelt

We all know that books burn—yet we have the greater knowledge that books cannot be killed by fire. People die, but books never die.

—Franklin D. Roosevelt

Censorship may be useful for the preservation of morality, but can never be so for its restoration.

—Jean Jacques Rousseau

The censors strive with a certain sadness in their hearts, for they feel that whatever they do the trouble cannot really be removed, only "regulated."

—William Ryan

Didn't we know all along that the censors are at best voyeurs?

—Robert Scheer

Assassination is the extreme form of censorship.

—George Bernard Shaw

Censorship reflects a society's lack of confidence in itself.

—Potter Stewart

If a man is pictured chopping off a woman's breast, it only gets an "R" rating; but if, God forbid, a man is pictured kissing a woman's breast, it gets an "X" rating. Why is violence more acceptable than tenderness?

—Sally Struthers

Any country that has sexual censorship will eventually have political censorship.

—Kenneth Tynan

It is the characteristic of the most stringent censorships that they give credibility to the opinions they attack.

—*Voltaire*

The censor's sword pierces deeply into the heart of free expression.

—*Earl Warren*

I believe in censorship. After all, I made a fortune from it.

—*Mae West*

God forbid that any book should be banned. The practice is as indefensible as infanticide.

—*Rebecca West*

Without censorship, things can get terribly confused in the public mind.

—*William Westmoreland, commander of U.S. forces in Vietnam*

The ACLU says it's wrong to take a child and make that child participate in the filming of child pornography, but once the molestation and abuse of the child is put on film, the distribution of the film is protected by the First Amendment. Such logic would say it's wrong to steal another man's money, but once you've stolen it you're free to spend it.

—*Donald Wildmon*

Government secrecy breeds stupidity, in government decision making and in the thinking of some citizens.

—*George Will*

See also *Freedom of Expression*

Columnists

It's a tragedy that all of the people who know how to run the country are newspaper columnists or TV commentators.

—Anonymous

Quotations are a columnist's bullpen. Stealing someone else's words frequently spares the embarrassment of eating your own.

—Peter Anderson

Columnists' tendency to spend their time with life's winners and to lead lives of isolation from the less dazzling American realities make it too easy for us sometimes to solve the nation's problems in 700 words.

—Russell Baker

It takes great self-confidence to write a newspaper column. Some might say it takes arrogance. Be that as it may, my willingness to pronounce on a great many matters of which I have little or no knowledge is one of my prime qualifications for this trade.

—Russell Baker

Political pundits can predict any old nonsense, and when it doesn't come true no one seems to mind.

—Craig Brown

Remember, you only have that space because some advertiser wouldn't buy it.

—Herb Caen, to columnists

A newspaper is known by the columnists it keeps.

—Irvin S. Cobb

[The columnist] must . . . have a well-stored mind and the integrated outlook of a man who has worked out his basic assumptions to the point where they give him a reasoned welt-anschauung. These attributes are necessarily rare. Yet without them a columnist is merely a performer, someone with technique and after that nothing.

—Charles Curran

Being a columnist is like being married to a nymphomaniac. Every time you think you're through, you have to start all over again.

—Ellen Goodman

I guess the thing that strikes me most is how the column consumes your life. It sounds as if it's just a job, but you find yourself being unable to make a distinction between the hours you're working and the hours that are allegedly your own.

—Bob Greene

If you lose your temper at a newspaper columnist, he'll get rich or famous or both.

—James C. Hagerty

Personal columnists are jackals and no jackal has been known to live on grass once he had learned about meat—no matter who killed the meat for him.

—Ernest Hemingway

The columnist's stock in trade is falsification and vilification. He is journalism's Public Enemy No. 1, and if the American press is to improve itself, it must get rid of him.

—Harold L. Ickes

The permanent power brokers of this city [Washington, D.C.] are the columnists.

—Hugh Newell Jacobsen

It's really difficult to get out of gossip columns once you've got in.

—Mick Jagger

If you want to get to the largest number of people, you try to get on television, but if you are trying to scuttle someone's program or get a hearing within the highest levels of the Administration, you go to a columnist.

—Ted Koppel

It is the gossip columnist's business to write about what is none of his business.

—Louis Kronenberger

A politician wouldn't dream of being allowed to call a columnist the things a columnist is allowed to call a politician.

—Max Lerner

A newspaper column, like a fish, should be consumed when fresh, otherwise it is not only indigestible, but unspeakable.

—James Reston

The most successful [newspaper] column is one that causes the reader to throw down the paper in a fit of pique.

—William Safire

In the 1930s the "column" became the dominant journalistic form, in which an assessment of what mattered in the public sphere was provided under the signature of an individual respected for his insight, his judgment and for being "in the know." . . . The columnist spoke with his own authority, which was above that of editors or publishers and which was self-legitimizing and mitigated only by other columnists with contradictory views.

—Anthony Smith

Columnist: A guy who finds things out that people do not want known, and tells them to people to whom it doesn't make any difference.

—Walter Winchell

Credibility, Accuracy and Bias

A story is only as good as the dumbest error in it.
> —*Anonymous city editor*

Remember, son, many a good story has been ruined by oververification.
> —*James Gordon Bennett Sr., advice to his son*

Get it first, but first get it right.
> —*Seymour Berkson*

If you want your name spelled wrong, die.
> —*Al Blanchard*

Unless we in the press move to resolve some [credibility] problems, we risk, over the long term, serious erosion of public acceptance of the basic First Amendment principles.
> —*Louis Boccardi*

A cross that journalism, especially *The Washington Post*, and especially Benjamin C. Bradlee, will bear forever.
> —*Ben Bradlee, on the fabrication in 1980 of a story for which reporter Janet Cooke won a Pulitzer Prize, which the paper then returned*

I do not mind lying but I hate inaccuracy.
> —*Samuel Butler*

It was long ago in my life as a simple reporter that I decided that facts must never get in the way of truth.

—*James Cameron*

Carney's Law: There's at least a 50–50 chance that someone will print the name Craney incorrectly.

—*Jim Canrey*

Most of the media's stories are accurate. My problem is that they are not complete.

—*David Demarest*

Accuracy of statement is one of the first elements of truth; inaccuracy is a near kin to falsehood.

—*Tryon Edwards*

The old argument that the networks and other "media elites" have a liberal bias is so blatantly true that it's hardly worth discussing any more. No, we don't sit around in dark corners and plan strategies on how we're going to slant the news. We don't have to. It comes naturally to most reporters.

—*Bernard Goldberg*

It has been my experience that what most viewers and readers are most unhappy about is not that journalists slant the news, but that we don't slant it their way.

—*Don Hewitt*

Facts do not cease to exist because they are ignored.

—*Aldous Huxley*

[M]any biases, most of them professional, not political, shape the news. Reporters have a bias toward the use of official sources, a bias toward information that can be obtained quickly, a bias toward conflict, a bias toward focusing on discreet events rather than persistent conditions, and a bias toward the simple over the complex.

—Kathleen Hall Jamieson and Paul Waldman

Once a newspaper touches a story, the facts are lost forever, even to the protagonists.

—Norman Mailer

I'll know my career's going bad when they start quoting me correctly.

—Lee Marvin

There are no facts, only interpretations.

—Friedrich Nietzsche

Early in life I noticed that no event is ever correctly reported in a newspaper.

—George Orwell

Facts speak for themselves.

—Plautus

Accuracy! Accuracy! Accuracy!

—Joseph Pulitzer

Accuracy is to a newspaper what virtue is to a woman.
—Joseph Pulitzer (see also Stevenson in this section)

Every story has three sides to it: yours, mine, and the facts.
—Foster Meharny Russell

A little inaccuracy sometimes saves tons of explanation.

—Saki

Neither in what it gives, nor in what it does not give, nor in the mode of presentation, must the unclouded face of truth suffer wrong. Comment is free but facts are sacred.

—C. P. Scott

Accuracy is to newspapers what virtue is to a lady, except that a newspaper can always print a retraction.

—Adlai Stevenson (see also Pulitzer in this section)

The first duty of a newspaper is to be accurate. If it be accurate, it follows that it is fair.

—Herbert Bayard Swope

Get your facts first, then you can distort them as you please.

—Mark Twain

It is necessary always to aim at being interesting rather than exact, for the spectator forgives everything except boredom.

—Voltaire

The truth is rarely pure, and never simple.

—Oscar Wilde

Readers remember mistakes longer than scoops.

—Thomas Winship

See also *Ethics, Values and Standards*

Critics and Reviewers

A critic is a bundle of biases held loosely together by a sense of taste.

> —*Whitney Balliett*

Reviewers seemed to fall into two classes: those who had little to say, and those who had nothing.

> —*Max Beerbohm*

Critics are like eunuchs in a harem: they know how it's done, they've seen it done every day, but they're unable to do it themselves.

> —*Brendan Behan*

I know how foolish critics can be, being one myself.

> —*Anthony Burgess*

I sometimes think
His critical judgment is so exquisite
It leaves us nothing to admire except his opinion.

> —*Christopher Fry*

Any fool can criticize—and many of them do.

> —*Cyril Garbett*

Critics make *pipi* on music and think they help it grow.

> —*Andre Gédalge*

TV criticism: Like trying to explain an accident.

—*Jackie Gleason*

It is a barren kind of criticism which tells you what a thing is not.

—*A. Whitney Griswold*

Asking a working writer what he thinks about critics is like asking a lamp-post how it feels about dogs.

—*Christopher Hampton*

A good review from the critics is just another stay of execution.

—*Dustin Hoffman*

Nature, when she invented, manufactured and patented her authors, contrived to make critics out of the chips that were left.

—*Oliver Wendell Holmes, Sr.*

A critic is a man who expects miracles.

—*James Gibbons Huneker*

The strength of criticism lies only in the weakness of the thing criticized.

—*Henry Wadsworth Longfellow*

People ask you for criticism, but they only want praise.

—*W. Somerset Maugham*

A drama critic is a person who surprises a playwright by informing him what he means.

—*Wilson Mizner*

A critic is a legless man who teaches running.

—*Channing Pollock*

Reviewmanship. . . "how to be one up on the author without actually tampering with the text." In other words how, as a critic, to show that it is really yourself who should have written the book, if you had had the time, and since you hadn't are glad that someone else has, although obviously it might have been done better.

—*Stephen Potter*

A drama critic is a man who leaves no turn unstoned.

—*George Bernard Shaw*

Pay no attention to what the critics say; there has never been a statue set up in honor of a critic.

—*Jean Sibelius*

A critic is a man who knows the way but can't drive the car.

—*Kenneth Tynan*

They search for ages for the wrong word which, to give them credit, they eventually find.

—*Peter Ustinov*

Democracy and the Media

Television is democracy at its ugliest.

—Paddy Chayefsky

Let's agree that while journalists have a vital role to play as watchdogs, they sometimes just plain get in the way of the most sacred transaction in a democracy—candidate to citizen.

—Walter Cronkite

The electronic democracy does not cancel out good journalism. It will, in fact, be dependent on good journalism. It won't work without good journalism.

—Leonard Downie Jr.

Democracy becomes a government of bullies tempered by editors.

—Ralph Waldo Emerson

The crucial role of journalism in a democracy is to provide a common ground of knowledge and analysis, a meeting place for national debate: It is the link between people and institutions.

—William A. Henry III

A democracy works best when the people have all the information that the security of the nation permits.

—Lyndon B. Johnson

The press is the weak slat under the bed of democracy.

—*A. J. Liebling*

Just as we are on the verge of another huge leap into the unknown—the total internationalization of news information—my biggest concern is this: how well are the astonishing leaps in media development serving the democracy and its institutions? Are we making miracles with our dazzling exploitations but *un*making in the process the best miracle man has yet invented for human happiness, the modern democratic state?

—*Robert MacNeil*

A popular government, without popular information, or the means of acquiring it, is but a prologue to a farce or a tragedy; or, perhaps, both. Knowledge will forever govern ignorance, and a people who mean to be their own governors must arm themselves with the power which knowledge gives.

—*James Madison*

One has to accept that democracy cannot function without the media.

—*Nelson Mandela*

[W]hen information which properly belongs to the public is systematically withheld by those in power, the people soon become ignorant of their own affairs, distrustful of those who manage them, and—eventually—incapable of determining their own destinies.

—*Richard M. Nixon*

Once the American public loses faith in the press as an institution of prime importance to the democratic process, then the most fundamental protection of the press—far greater than the embodied First Amendment—will have been lost.

—*John Oakes*

No longer are we [journalists] just the messengers, observers on the sidelines, witch's mirrors faithfully telling society how it looks. Now we are deeply embedded in the democratic process itself, as principal actors rather than bit players or mere audience.

—Mike O'Neill

Television has made dictatorship impossible, but democracy unbearable.

—Shimon Peres

Media which are not free to criticize the government, or that are not representative of the broad spectrum of society, are inherently limited in their capacity to support and bolster democracy.

—Cyril Ramaphosa, South African media executive

Journalists in the United States are at a critical point in the history of their craft. Threatened on one side by declining readership and new economic pressures in the media industry, they face a different kind of threat from fraying of community ties, the rising disgust with politics, and a spreading sense of impotence and hopelessness among Americans frustrated by the failures of their democratic system. If this second threat isn't noticed and taken seriously, American journalism may lose control of its future, which is bound up with the strength of public life in all its forms.

—Jay Rosen and Davis "Buzz" Merritt

We are moving from a parliamentary democracy to a television democracy.

—Helmut Schmidt

See also *Government and the Media; Politics, Politicians and the Media; Presidents and the Media*

Editorials

So barons of the press who know their readers
Employ to write their more appalling leaders,
Instead of Satan's horrid and hideous minions
Clever young men of liberal opinions.

—*W. H. Auden, 1937*

Writing good editorials is chiefly telling the people what *they* think, not what *you* think.

—*Arthur Brisbane*

The reader deserves an honest opinion. If he doesn't deserve it, give it to him anyhow.

—*John Ciardi*

God protect you against brilliant people. Brilliant people belong writing editorials. You know, they don't make good reporters, they invent too much. But they are wonderful editorial writers. Nobody knows better what to tell Mrs. Gandhi on how to run India than an editorial writer. And it's harmless because they will never be called on to do anything about it.

—*Peter Drucker*

Editorial writers . . . enter after the battle and shoot the wounded.

—*Neil Goldschmidt*

I get very provocative in an editorial. I can't stand apple pie and that kind of stuff; I think an editorial has to be strong, very dogmatic, very provocative. There's too much fluff in editorials everywhere.

—*Norman Runnion*

Often his editorial policy was a nice compromise between blackmail and begging.

—*William Allen White, on a fellow editor*

Editors and Editing

Assistant City Editor: A mouse learning to be a rat.

—Anonymous

An editor knocked at the Pearly Gates,
Her face was scarred and cold;
She stood before the man of fate
for admission to the Fold.
"What have you done?" St. Peter asked,
To gain admission here?"
"I've been an editor, sir," she said
As she shed a tear.

The Pearly Gates swung open wide,
St. Peter touched the bell—
"Come in," he said, "and choose your harp,
You've had your share of hell."

—Anonymous

Always remember that if editors were so damned smart, they would know how to dress.

—Dave Barry

In the old days, stories were checked by editors before being printed; today, editors are busy doing surveys on declining journalism credibility, so they have no time to look at the actual publication.

—Dave Barry

Would you convey my compliments to the purist who reads your proofs and tell him or her that I write in a sort of broken-down patois which is something like the way a Swiss waiter talks, and that when I split an infinitive, God damn it, I split it so it will stay split.

—*Raymond Chandler*

A man who knows what he wants but doesn't know what it is.

—*Walter Davenport*

Being an editor is a hard job, but a fascinating one. There's nothing so hard as minding your own business and an editor never has to do that.

—*Finley Peter Dunne*

An editor should tell the writer his writing is better than it is. Not a lot better, a little better.

—*T. S. Eliot*

Yes, I suppose some editors are failed writers—but so are most writers.

—*T. S. Eliot*

An editor should have a pimp for a brother, so he'd have someone to look up to.

—*Gene Fowler*

An "editor" should be qualified with an extensive acquaintance with languages, a great easiness and command of writing and relating things clearly and intelligibly, and in few words; he should be able to speak of war both by land and sea; be well-acquainted with geography, with the history of time, with the several interests of princes and states, the secrets of courts, and the manners and customs of all nations.

—*Benjamin Franklin*

Editors may think of themselves as dignified headwaiters in a well-run restaurant but more often [they] operate a snack bar . . . and expect you to be grateful that at least they got the food to the table warm.

—Thomas Griffith

Editing: A bit of sandpaper applied to all forms of originality.
—Elbert Hubbard

[An editor is] a person employed on a newspaper, whose business it is to separate the wheat from the chaff, and see that the chaff is printed.
—Elbert Hubbard (also attributed to Adlai Stevenson)

Hand-holding, fostering, pruning, snipping, squelching, and encouraging have always been the true functions of the editor.
—Ernst Jacobi

[T]he author is always the boss. . . . The editor has one and only one job: to help the author write precisely what the author wants to write in the best way possible.
—Derrick Jensen

The trick to editing . . . is to find out where the other person's heart resides, and then help him or her to get there.
—Derrick Jensen

Read your own compositions, and when you meet with a passage which you think is particularly fine, strike it out.
—Samuel Johnson

An editor is a man who takes a French poodle, and clips him into the shape of a lion.

—Emery Kelen

To read almost any American daily today is to conclude that copy editors have vanished as completely from our city rooms as the ivory-billed woodpecker has from the southern woodlands. We appear to have reared a generation of young reporters whose mastery of spelling, to put the matter mildly, is something less than nil. . . . Once there was a white-haired geezer in an eyeshade to intercept a reporter's copy, and to explain gently but firmly to the author that *phase* and *faze* are different words, and that *affect* and *effect* ought not to be confused. The old geezer has gone and literacy with him.

—James J. Kilpatrick

The difference between managing and editing is that a word doesn't tell you to go f*** yourself when you tell it to move.

—Louise Kohl

We have a reasonably free press in this country, but there are far too many captive editors who cannot even be heard to rattle their chains.

—Carl E. Lindstrom

A good editor has a sharp nose for what to put into a newspaper and an even sharper nose for what to leave out.

—Judy Mann

I notice what you say about your aspiration to edit a magazine. I am sending you by this mail a six-chambered revolver. Load it and fire every one into your head. You will thank me when you get to hell and learn from other editors there how dreadful their job was on earth.

—H. L. Mencken, in a letter to William Saroyan

"Sixty Horses Wedged in Chimney"
The story to fit this sensational headline has not turned up yet.

—J. B. Morton

Every reporter is a hope; every editor is a disappointment.

—Joseph Pulitzer

Editing is the same as quarreling with writers—same thing exactly.

—Harold Ross

An editor has no friends.

—Jack Tanner

I am not an editor of a newspaper, and shall always try to do right and be good so that God will not make me one.

—Mark Twain

No passion in the world is equal to the passion to alter someone else's draft.

—H. G. Wells

An editor is a person who knows more about writing than writers do but who has escaped the terrible desire to write.

—E. B. White

I became the editor of a weekly newspaper because I wanted to be my own particular kind of damn fool.

—William Allen White

Ethics, Values and Standards

If the press has values it cares about, it should articulate them lest it be understood as having no values at all.

—Floyd Abrams

The entire media business has lost its [ethical] moorings. The Internet does not play by the same rules as old-fashioned journalists do, and since it seems to be winning the battle for the young audience, the old guys are throwing out their old rule books without bothering to write a new one.

—Eric Alterman

In recent years, journalism has moved beyond the most unintelligent strictures of objectivity, substituting instead the ideas of fairness and balance. A competent journalist is no longer expected to remain passive when an authority figure utters a "fact" for which there is documented contrary evidence. But there persists the illusion throughout American journalism that it operates as a value-free discipline.

—Ben Bagdikian

Vilify! Vilify! Some of it will always stick.

—Pierre-Augustin Beaumarchais

Journalists say a thing they know isn't true, in the hope that if they keep on saying it long enough, it *will* be true.

—Arnold Bennett

There are those who think journalism ethics is an oxymoron.

—Bob Berg

The higher profile the story, the lower the ethics.

—Jack Briggs

If I were objective or if you were objective or if anyone was, he would have to be put away somewhere in an institution because he'd be some sort of vegetable.

—David Brinkley

Truth-tellers are not always palatable. There is a preference for candy bars.

—Gwendolyn Brooks

The humbug and hypocrisy of the press begin only when the newspapers pretend to be "impartial" or "servants of the public." And this becomes dangerous as well as laughable when the public is fool enough to believe it.

—Claud Cockburn

The press must also be accountable. It must be accountable to society for meeting the public need and for maintaining the rights of citizens and the almost forgotten rights of speakers who have no press. It must know that its faults and errors have ceased to be private vagaries and have become public dangers.

—Commission on Freedom of the Press, 1947

The characteristics of the American journalist consist in an open mind and coarse appeal to the passions of his readers; he abandons principles to assail the characters of individuals, to track them into private life, and disclose all their weaknesses and vices.

—Alexis de Tocqueville

Journalism without a moral position is impossible. Every journalist is a moralist. It's absolutely unavoidable.

—Marguerite Duras

Pursuit of truth is not a license to be a jerk.

—Jack Fuller

Ethics and morals . . . [have] nothing to do with breaking a story and getting it in the paper. There are only two rules of real newspapering: get the story, get it out. All the rest is up to private conscience.

—Bill Granger

Don't be afraid to make a mistake, your readers might like it.

—William Randolph Hearst

There were no responsibilities beyond enthusiasm.

—Ben Hecht, on U.S. journalism in 1910

One sacred rule of journalism: The writer must not invent. The legend on the license must read: *None of this was made up.* The ethics of journalism, if we can be allowed such a boon, must be based on the simple truth that every journalist knows the difference between the distortion that comes from subtracting observed data and the distortion that comes from adding invented data.

—John Hersey

Good taste is, of course, an utterly dispensable part of any journalist's equipment.

—Michael Hogg

I'm so saturated by the irresponsibility of the media that I'm beyond being outraged. I'm almost numb at this point.

—Lance Ito, judge in the O. J. Simpson trial

We enjoy the shield of the First Amendment, but it can't, won't and shouldn't protect us from any resentment we engender when we act as if we were accountable only to ourselves and as if we had no obligation at all to the public.

—*Colbert King*

Everything you read in the newspaper is absolutely true except for that rare story of which you happen to have firsthand knowledge.

—*Erwin Knoll*

Most newspaper writers regard truth as their most valuable possession, and therefore are most economical in its use.

—*Leonard Louis Levenson*

The theory of a free press is that the truth will emerge from free reporting and free discussions, not that it will be presented perfectly and instantly in any one account.

—*Walter Lippmann*

Journalists can't meet high-tech, high-diversity, high-profile modern news challenges with horse-and-buggy ethics.

—*Austin Long-Scott*

Show me a man who claims to be objective and I'll show you a man with illusions.

—*Henry R. Luce*

Political cartoonists violate every rule of ethical journalism—they misquote, trifle with the truth, make science fiction out of politics. . . . But when the smoke clears, the political cartoonist has been getting closer to the truth than the guy who writes political opinions.

—*Jeff MacNelly*

Every journalist who is not too stupid or too full of himself to notice what is going on knows that what he does is morally indefensible.

—Janet Malcolm

Ethics are what publishers say they are.

—Art Nauman

I am a journalist and, under the modern journalist's code of Olympian objectivity (and total purity of motive), I am absolved of responsibility. We journalists don't have to step on roaches. All we have to do is turn on the kitchen light and watch the critters scurry.

—P. J. O'Rourke

The ethical reporter who is committed to truth will inevitably be drawn in whatever story he or she is covering to the dimensions of justice, peace and morality, for the dynamic of truth yields justice and peace.

—Wes Pippert

The high-minded in the [journalism] business attempting to teach their morals to the fast and loose at the popular end . . . stand as much chance of having an impact as someone trying to advocate celibacy to a group of sailors arriving home in port after six months at sea.

—David Randall

If editors and journalists insist on accuracy, professionalism, and sensitivity in reporting, the public will likely support a free press in the broadest sense.

—Bruce W. Sanford

We're in the same position as a plumber laying a pipe. We're not responsible for what goes through the pipe.

—David Sarnoff

Members of the Society of Professional Journalists believe that public enlightenment is the forerunner of justice and the foundation of democracy. The duty of the journalist is to further those ends by seeking truth and providing a fair and comprehensive account of events and issues. Conscientious journalists from all media and specialties strive to serve the public with thoroughness and honesty. Professional integrity is the cornerstone of a journalist's credibility. Members of the Society share a dedication to ethical behavior and adopt this code to declare the Society's principles and standards of practice.

—Society of Professional Journalists'
Code of Ethics, preamble, 1996

The ethics of journalism are the same as the ethics for living.
—Jim Wooten

See also *Credibility, Accuracy and Bias; The First Amendment; Freedom of Expression; Law*

The First Amendment

A lot of people think that the First Amendment was only the first one written, and that they got better as they went along.

—David Bartlett

The First Amendment stands for the notion that when it comes to free speech and a free press, government is always the problem, never the solution.

—David Bartlett

An unconditional right to say what one pleases about public affairs is what I consider to be the minimum guarantee of the First Amendment.

—Hugo Black

The First Amendment does not speak equivocally. It prohibits any law abridging freedom of speech or of the press. It must be taken as a command of the broadest scope that explicit language, read in the context of a liberty-loving society, will allow.

—Hugo Black

You cannot tamper with the First Amendment. The moment you tamper with it, it falls apart.

—Alistair Cooke

I don't think the way to make the point that the First Amendment is important is to [honor] the most outrageous abuses of that great privilege.

—Mario Cuomo

Socialists . . . have come to realize . . . that it is extremely dangerous to exercise the constitutional right of free speech in a country fighting to make democracy safe in the world.

—Eugene V. Debs, 1918

Just as booksellers have a First Amendment right to sell whatever they please, they have a First Amendment right to refrain from selling that which they find objectionable.

—Morris Dees

The First Amendment didn't say that we should not abridge a responsible press, it just said "the press."

—Millicent Fenwick

The First Amendment is an essential part of cultural policy because it gives the artist, the thinker, the social commentator, the right to speak freely without . . . intellectual restraint of any kind.

—John Frohnmayer

I sometimes believe that we journalists use the First Amendment the way a diplomat uses his passport when he's stopped for drunk driving.

—Jeff Greenfeld

The First Amendment presupposes that right conclusions are more likely to be gathered out of a multitude of tongues, than through any kind of authoritative selection. To many this is, and always will be, folly; but we have staked upon it our all.

—Learned Hand

Freedom is always the exception, never the rule. Of all human beings who have lived on this earth, only a few have lived in freedom. For the anonymous millions living private lives in this country today, the First Amendment, above all else, is the constitutional expression in their behalf of the greatest of all human values: Freedom of the mind.

—Philip Kerby

Deserve the First Amendment.

—Journalists' slogan; source unknown

Anytime I hear people waving the First Amendment, I remind them of the 21st Amendment—the short one that abolished prohibition and says that the 18th Amendment is hereby repealed.

—Paul Poorman

The First Amendment requires that we protect some falsehood in order to protect speech that matters.

—Lewis Powell Jr.

I admit the constitutional right of the rappers and the hip-hoppers to their foul language. . . . I admit the constitutional right of the record companies to earn serious money by producing and marketing such trash. But some things that are entirely constitutional are nonetheless deadly. . . . Neither the First Amendment nor common sense requires us to be parties to our own degradation.

—William Raspberry

In public debate our own citizens must tolerate insulting, and even outrageous, speech in order to provide adequate breathing space to the freedoms protected by the First Amendment.

—William Rehnquist

The First Amendment is a very liberal amendment as it is now applied and interpreted. . . . That liberality depends to a large extent upon the responsibility with which the freedom that it confers is exercised. Since the ultimate law of any society is going to be survival, if that responsibility disappears, other statutes will be passed.

—Antonin Scalia

The primary purpose of the constitutional guarantee of a free press was to create a fourth institution outside the government as an additional check on the three official branches.

—Potter Stewart

The Founding Fathers thought that liberty was more important than fairness, so they adopted the First Amendment.

—Tom Tauke

Congress shall make no law respecting an establishment of religion, or prohibiting the free exercise thereof; or abridging the freedom of speech or of the press; or the right of the people peacefully to assemble, and to petition the government for a redress of grievances.

—U.S. Constitution, First Amendment

I don't think it's fair to blame the First Amendment when someone makes a fool of himself in public.

—Mary Worth, cartoon character

See also *Freedom of Expression; Law*

Freedom of Expression

It is not merely the fine language of special pleaders when we say that freedom of the press is a basic freedom—yes, the basic freedom. Without it no other freedom can long exist.

—M. V. Atwood

If you want a watchdog to warn you of intruders, you must put up with a certain amount of mistakened barking. Now and then he will sound off because a stray dog seems to be invading his territory . . . or because he is outraged by a postman, and that kind of barking can, of course, be a nuisance. But if you muzzle him and leash him and teach him decorum, you will find that he doesn't do the job for which you got him in the first place. Some extraneous barking is the price you must pay for his service as a watchdog. A free press is the watchdog of a free society. And only a press free enough to be somewhat irresponsible can possibly fulfill this vital function.

—Alan Barth

I'm all in favor of free expression provided it's kept rigidly under control.

—Alan Bennett

The liberty of the press is indeed essential to the nature of a free state, but this consists in laying no previous restraints upon publications, and not in freedom from censure for criminal matter when published.

—William Blackstone, 1765

If the press is not free, if speech is not independent and un-trammeled, if the mind is shackled or made impotent through fear, it makes no difference under what form of government you live, you are a subject and not a citizen.

—William E. Borah

If there be time to expose through discussion the falsehoods and the fallacies, to avert the evil by the process of education, the remedy to be applied is more speech not enforced silence.

—Louis Brandeis

True, many criticisms may be, like their authors, devoid of good taste, but better all sorts of criticism than no criticism at all.

—David Brewer

Almost nobody means precisely what he says when he makes the declaration, "I'm in favor of free speech."

—Heywood Broun

Everybody favors free speech in the slack moments when no axes are being ground.

—Heywood Broun

A free press can of course be good or bad, but, most certainly, without freedom it will never be anything but bad.

—Albert Camus

Ultimately, the people will have just as much freedom of speech as they want.

—Zechariah Chafee Jr.

The majority of us are for free speech only when it deals with those subjects concerning which we have no intense convictions.

—Edmund B. Chaffee

In Canada, we respect freedom of speech, but we don't worship it.

—*Ronald I. Cohen, Chair of the*
Canadian Broadcast Standards Council

A king of England has an interest in preserving the freedom of the press, because it is his interest to know the true state of the nation, which the courtiers would fain conceal, but of which a free press can alone inform him.

—*C. C. Colton*

An enslaved press is doubly fatal; it not only takes away the true light, for in that case we might stand still, but it sets up a false one that decoys us to our destruction.

—*C. C. Colton*

The justification and the purpose of freedom of speech is not to indulge those who want to speak their minds. It is to prevent error and discover truth. There may be other ways of detecting error and discovering truth than that of free discussion, but so far we have not found them.

—*Henry Steele Commager*

In order to enjoy the inestimable benefits that the liberty of the press ensures, it is necessary to submit to the inevitable evils that it creates.

—*Alexis de Tocqueville*

The most beautiful thing in the world is freedom of speech.

—*Diogenes*

Acceptance by government of a dissident press is a measure of the maturity of a nation.

—*William O. Douglas*

Free speech is the rule, not the exception.

—*William O. Douglas*

When ideas compete in the market for acceptance, full and free discussion [exposes] the false and they gain few adherents. Full and free discussion even of ideas we hate encourages the testing of our own prejudices and preconceptions. Full and free discussion keeps a society from being stagnant and unprepared for the stress and strains that work to tear all civilizations apart.

—William O. Douglas

It is the central, defining premise of freedom of speech that the offensiveness of ideas, or the challenge they offer to traditional ideas, cannot be a valid reason for censorship; once that premise is abandoned, it is difficult to see what free speech means.

—Ronald Dworkin

One of the many things that separates our society from [others] is our absolute right to propagate opinions that our government finds wrong or even hateful.

—Frank Hoover Easterbrook

Dissidence ought to be regarded as one of our finest traditions and proudest exports to the world.

—Barbara Ehrenreich

Whereas democracy will be destroyed if it is not practiced, the same can be said of a free press. It must be put to use and defended, no matter what the cost, or else it will erode to nothing.

—Dan Ehrlich

Freedom of the press . . . is not an end in itself but a means to the end of a free society.

—Felix Frankfurter

One of the prerogatives of American citizenship is the right to criticize public men and measures—that means not only informed and responsible criticism, but also the right to speak foolishly and without moderation.

—Felix Frankfurter

Abuses of the freedom of speech ought to be repressed, but to whom dare we commit the power of doing it?

—*Benjamin Franklin*

Printers are educated in the belief that when men differ in opinion both sides ought equally to have the advantage of being heard by the public; and that when truth and error have fair play, the former is always an overmatch for the latter: hence they cheerfully serve all contending writers that pay them well, without regarding on which side they are of the question in dispute.

—*Benjamin Franklin*

Newspapers, if they are to be interesting, must not be molested.

—*Frederick the Great*

Freedom is not worth having if it does not connote freedom to err.

—*Mahatma Gandhi*

It is the abhorrent and awful speech that needs to be protected. Nice and polite words can take care of themselves.

—*Michael Gartner*

The freedom of speech and the freedom of the press have not been granted to the people in order that they may say things which please, but [that they have] the right to say the things which displease.

—*Samuel Gompers*

We have a professional responsibility to be right, and a constitutional right to be wrong.

—*Robert Green*

The failings are our own. We are, indeed, very free, but we do not use our freedoms enough. We accommodate to power, and we have done so for far too long.

—*David Halberstam*

What is the Liberty of the Press? Who can give it any definition which does not leave the utmost latitude for evasion? I hold it to be impracticable, and from this I infer that its security, whatever fine declarations may be inserted in any constitution respecting it, must altogether depend on public opinion, and on the general spirit of the people and the government.

—Alexander Hamilton

Freedom of speech does not give a person the right to shout "Fire!" in a crowded theater.

—Oliver Wendell Holmes Jr.

The very aim and end of our institutions is just this: that we may think what we like and say what we like.

—Oliver Wendell Holmes Sr.

The right to be heard does not automatically include the right to be taken seriously.

—Hubert H. Humphrey

The primary responsibility of safeguarding a free press lies, and will continue to lie, upon the press itself.

—Cushrow R. Irani, Indian editor

A free press is the first activity attacked or shut up by those who fear the investigation of their actions.

—Thomas Jefferson

Equal and exact justice to all men . . . freedom of religion, freedom of the press, freedom of person under habeas corpus; and trial by juries impartially selected. These principles form the bright constellation which has gone before us and guided our steps through an age of revolution and reformation.

—Thomas Jefferson, First inaugural address, 1801

The only security of all is in a free press.

—Thomas Jefferson

People hardly ever make use of the freedom they have, for example, freedom of thought; instead, they demand freedom of speech as a compensation.

—*Sören Kierkegaard*

A free press is usually among the first victims of an angry and frustrated society. As social problems increase, there will be the inevitable calls for controls on the news media.

—*Ted Koppel*

Liberals don't much like commercial speech because it's commercial; conservatives mistrust it because it's speech.

—*Alex Kozinski*

Why should freedom of speech and freedom of the press be allowed? Why should a government which is doing what it believes to be right allow itself to be criticized? It would not allow opposition by lethal weapons. Ideas are much more fatal things than guns. Why should any man be allowed to buy a printing press and disseminate pernicious opinions calculated to embarrass the government?

—*Nikolai Lenin*

The liberty of thinking and of publishing whatever one likes . . . is the fountainhead of many evils.

—*Pope Leo XIII*

Freedom of the press is guaranteed only to those who own one.

—*A. J. Liebling*

Let the people know the facts, and the country will be safe.

—*Abraham Lincoln*

A free press is not a privilege but an organic necessity in a great society.

—*Walter Lippmann*

The right of free speech belongs to those who are willing to preserve it.

—*Walter Lippmann*

Freedom of speech is better than sex.

—*Madonna*

The freedom of the press is one of the great bulwarks of liberty, and can never be restrained but by despotic governments.

—*George Mason*

What is essential is not that everyone shall speak, but that everything worth saying shall be said.

—*Alexander Meiklejohn*

It ought not to be permitted to speak well of public functionaries without an equal liberty of speaking ill.

—*James Mill*

If all mankind, minus one, were of one opinion, and only one person were of the contrary opinion, mankind would be no more justified in silencing that one person than he, if he had the power, would be justified in silencing mankind.

—*John Stuart Mill*

Give me the liberty to know, to utter and to argue freely according to conscience, above all liberties.

—*John Milton*

Though all the winds of doctrine were let loose upon the earth, so Truth be in the field, we do ingloriously, by licensing and prohibiting, to misdoubt her strength. Let her and Falsehood grapple: who ever knew Truth put the worse in a free and open encounter?

—*John Milton*

When a person goes to a country and finds their newspapers filled with nothing but good news, he can bet there are good men in jail.

—*Daniel P. Moynihan*

Long experience has taught us that it is dangerous in the interest of truth to suppress opinions and ideas; it has further taught us that it is foolish to imagine that we can do so. It is far easier to meet an evil in the open and defeat it in fair combat in people's minds, than to drive it underground and have no hold on it or proper approach to it. Evil flourishes far more in the shadows than in the light of day.

—*Jawaharlal Nehru*

People believe that having freedom of expression is a natural phenomenon. It's not. It's the result of intense care and vigilance.

—*Burt Neuborne*

We cannot silence the voices that we do not like hearing. We can, however, do anything in our power to make certain that other voices are heard.

—*Deborah Prothrow-Stith*

It is a great deal better to err a little bit on the side of having too much discussion and having too virulent language used by the press, rather than to err on the side of having them not say what they ought to say, especially with reference to public men and measures.

—*Theodore Roosevelt*

Freedom of the press, once proclaimed, admits to no logical limit.

—*Vermont Royster*

When you allow limits on [freedom of the press], you think you are giving away 1 percent of your freedom and you think you still have 99 percent left, but it's amazing how quickly you lose that other 99 percent.

—Salmon Rushdie

The fundamental argument for freedom of opinion is the doubt fulness of all our beliefs.

—Bertrand Russell

Freedom of the press will become more and more an issue and the press will turn to public opinion for support against any onslaughts—perhaps only to find that no real public support exists.

—Lois Smallwood

The key to security is public information.

—Margaret Chase Smith

We accept the risk that words and ideas have wings that we cannot clip and which carry them we know not where.

—Joseph P. Sneed

My definition of a free society is a society where it is safe to be unpopular.

—Adlai Stevenson

The sound of tireless voices is the price we pay for the right to hear the music of our own opinions.

—Adlai Stevenson

A free but badly performing press serves its people far better than an efficient, government-controlled press.

—Leonard R. Sussman

A free press stands as one of the great interpreters between the government and the people. To allow it to be fettered is to fetter ourselves.

—George Sutherland

Where liberty has fallen, no one dares speak freely.

—*Publilius Syrus*

Everyone has the right to freedom of opinion and expression; this right includes freedom to hold opinions without interference and to seek, receive and impart information and ideas through any media regardless of frontiers.

—*Universal Declaration of Human Rights*

I disapprove of what you say, but I will defend to the death your right to say it.

—*Voltaire (attributed; nowhere did he say exactly these words, which may be a loose paraphrase of his views in his* Essay on Tolerance*: "Think for yourself, and let others enjoy the privilege to do so, too.")*

Our entire revolution was created by a free press and free thought.

—*Lech Walesa*

I am inordinately proud these days of the quill, for it has shown itself, historically, to be the hypodermic which inoculates men and keeps the germs of freedom always in circulation, so that there are individuals in every time in every land who are the carriers, the Typhoid Mary's, capable of infecting others by mere contact and example. These persons are feared by every tyrant—who shows his fear by burning the books and destroying the individuals.

—*E. B. White*

You say that freedom of utterance is not for time of stress, and I reply with the sad truth that only in time of stress is freedom of utterance in danger. No one questions it in calm days, because it is not needed.

—*William Allen White*

The whole point of free speech is not to make ideas exempt from criticism but to expose them to it.

—*Garry Wills*

See also *Censorship; The First Amendment*

Freelance

A freelance is one who gets paid by the word—per piece or perhaps.

—Robert Benchley

What an author likes to write most is his signature on the back of a cheque.

—Brendan Francis

There's no money in poetry, but then there's no poetry in money either.

—Robert Graves

Manuscript: something submitted in haste and returned at leisure.

—Oliver Herford

No man but a blockhead ever wrote except for money.

—Samuel Johnson

A good many young writers make the mistake of enclosing a stamped, self-addressed envelope, big enough for the manuscript to come back in. This is too much of a temptation to the editor.

—Ring Lardner

The writer must earn money in order to be able to live and to write, but he must by no means live and write for the purpose of making money.

—Karl Marx

Writing is like prostitution. First you do it for the love of it, then you do it for a few friends, and finally you do it for money.

—Ferenc Molnár

The two most beautiful words in the English language are "check enclosed."

—Dorothy Parker

The dubious privilege of a freelance writer is he's given the freedom to starve anywhere.

—S. J. Perlman

If Moses had been paid newspaper rates for the Ten Commandments, he might have written the Two Thousand Commandments.

—Isaac Bashevis Singer

Write without pay until somebody offers pay. If nobody offers within three years, the candidate may look upon this circumstance with the most implicit confidence as the sign that sawing wood is what he was intended for.

—Mark Twain

Write out of love; write out of instinct; write out of reason. But always for money.

—Louis Untermeyer

Poets are terribly sensitive people, and one of the things they are most sensitive about is cash.

—Robert Penn Warren

See also *Writers and Writing*

Government and the Media

Those of us on the outside looking in at government assume that policy is the product of rational decision-making by a handful of men, just as those outside newspapers looking in assume that news is the product of rational decision-making by a handful of men.

—Ben H. Bagdikian

The government's power to censor the press was abolished so the press would remain forever free to censure the government.

—Hugo Black

In moments of stress between government and the press, the government looks for ways to control the press, to eliminate or minimize the press as an obstacle in the implementation of policy, or the solution of problems. In these moments, especially, the press must continue its mission of publishing information that it—and it alone—determines to be in the public interest, in a useful, timely and responsible manner—serving society, not government.

—Benjamin Bradlee

Our primary obligation is to our readers. I wouldn't know how to interpret our obligation to the government.

—Turner Catledge

I think a lot of journalists think they could do a better job of running the country than anyone in office.

—Everette E. Dennis

The press must be free; it has always been so and much evil has been corrected by it. If government finds itself annoyed by it, let it examine its own conduct [to] find the cause.

—Thomas Erskine

[The news media] celebrate failure and ignore success. Nothing about government is done as incompetently as the reporting of it.

—Barney Frank

The quality of legislation passed to deal with a problem is inversely proportional to the volume of media clamor that brought it on.

—G. Ray Funkhouser

There is a terrific disadvantage not to have the abrasive quality of the press applied to you daily, to an administration, even though we never like it, and even though we wish they didn't write it, and even though we disapprove, there isn't any doubt that we could not do the job at all in a free society without a very, very active press.

—John F. Kennedy

Complete publicity makes it impossible to govern. No one has understood that better than the daily press; for no power has watched more carefully over the secret of its whole organization . . . [and] then continually cries out that the *government* should be quite public. Quite right; the intention of the press was to do away with government—and then itself govern . . .

—Sören Kierkegaard

Trying to conform to the government's definition of "responsible journalism" is a recipe for disaster.

—Jane Kirtley

Without criticism and reliable and intelligent reporting, the government cannot govern.

—Walter Lippmann

How can a government expect to govern without controlling television?

—André Malraux

It's [the government's] job to keep secrets. It's our job to find out about them.

—Walter Mears

If I loosened the reins on the press, I would not stay in power three months.

—Napoleon

Our republic and its press will rise or fall together.

—Joseph Pulitzer

The men with the muckrakes are often indispensable to the well-being of society; but only if they know when to stop raking the muck, and look upward to the celestial crown above them, to the crown of worthy endeavor. There are beautiful things above and around them; and if they gradually grow to feel that the whole world is nothing but muck, their power of usefulness is gone.

—Theodore Roosevelt

They didn't let them within one hundred yards of the building. That's what the founding fathers in Philadelphia thought of the press.

—Alan K. Simpson

The press has become the greatest power within western countries, more powerful than the legislature, the executive and the judiciary. One would then like to ask: by what law has it been elected and to whom is it responsible?

—Alexander Solzhenitsyn

For those who govern, the first thing required is indifference to newspapers.

—Louis Adolphe Thiers

Once a government is committed to a principle of silencing the voice of opposition, it has only one way to go, and that is down the path of increasingly repressive measures.

—Harry S. Truman

Electronic journalism enhances the power of spin doctors, flacks and media consultants to obfuscate and conceal and to clothe a great many naked emperors.

—Bernard A. Weisberger

See also *Democracy and the Media; Politics, Politicians and the Media; Presidents and the Media*

Internet

[The creation of the Internet] is one of the most profound communications events in the history of man.

—*James L. Barksdale*

When browsing the Web, you will almost certainly encounter lengthy delays, which means that it's a good idea to have something else to do while you're waiting, such as reroofing your house.

—*Dave Barry*

Consumers will be able to participate in the news process. Journalism will become less of a lecture and more of a conversation. Journalists will spend less time guessing what their customers might want to know and more time packaging and organizing an almost infinite body of raw material into reliable and useful information packages. More separate news organizations will appear, each a good deal smaller and more specialized than those we see today. . . . To survive in this more demanding and competitive environment, news producers will have to find new ways to profit from smaller shares of the total audience.

—*David Bartlett*

An electronic information highway that's jammed with the likes of Jimmy Swaggert, Madonna and Ice-T can easily be a road to nowhere.

—*Leo Bogart*

The Internet is an elite organization; most of the population of the world has never even made a phone call.

—*Noam Chomsky*

The superhighway needs sherpas and guides. . . . Use the Net if you must. Exploit the various new forms of distributing information. But remember this, the most adept collectors of information, the best organizers and electors of information, the best explainers of information, the best analyzers of information, are print journalists.

—*Peter Cole*

For many businesses, the Internet is still a technology in search of a strategy.

—*Mary J. Cronin*

I believe that if there is anything that would in any way tamper with freedom of speech or the press on the Internet, it should not be tolerated, and should end immediately. . . . However, I do believe that the use of the Internet should not be anonymous, that those who use the Internet must identify themselves with name and address, they should be reachable and they should be held responsible the same way everybody else who distributes information is held responsible for libel and slander.

—*Walter Cronkite*

As the most participatory form of mass speech yet developed, the Internet deserves the highest protection from governmental intrusion.

—*Stewart R. Dalzell*

The degree to which people can benefit from the Internet's potential for democratization, bring about true decentralization, or spread knowledge and education will depend on how much support the information-poor get to log on.

—*Kunda Dixit*

We have entered an era vibrating with the din of small voices. Every citizen can be a reporter, can take on the powers that be. . . . The Net gives as much voice to a thirteen-year-old computer geek . . . as to a CEO or Speaker of the House. We all become equal. . . . Now, with a modem, anyone can follow the world and report on the world—no middle man, no big brother.

—Matt Drudge

The growth of the Net is not a fluke or a fad, but the consequence of unleashing the power of individual creativity. If it were an economy, it would be the triumph of the free market over central planning. In music, jazz over Bach. Democracy over dictatorship.

—The Economist

The Net still resembles a congested street: Because users pay only for their car and fuel, rather than for the inconvenience their presence on the road imposes on others, they have no incentive to limit the use of their car to avoid traffic jams.

—The Economist

Cybermedia will make every man his own editor, which in turn makes every writer a fool. The Internet will transmit misinformation very efficiently. We will miss the gatekeepers.

—Neal B. Freeman

A fundamental new rule for business is that the Internet changes everything.

—Bill Gates

The Internet is becoming the town square for the global village of tomorrow.

—Bill Gates

The Internet is the first medium that allows anyone with reasonably inexpensive equipment to publish to a wide audience. It is the first medium that distributes information globally at almost no marginal cost.

—Bill Gates

As the PC gains communications powers and evolves into a teleputer, its social, cultural, and political impacts completely change. As it ushers in a life beyond TV, it becomes a powerful force for democracy, individuality, community, and high culture.

—George Gilder

No one could have predicted that computers would turn out to be a vast communications tool. They're empowering individuals in a way that no mass medium has ever done before. . . . I'm very upbeat about it, except for the fact that because it's immensely empowering, it's also immensely threatening, and a lot of different wings of government feel a need to step in and control it.

—Mike Godwin

[The Internet] ends the monopolies the power elite have long held in defining public debate.

—Mike Godwin

[The Internet is] the most participatory form of mass speech yet developed . . . a never-ending worldwide conversation.

—The Guardian

The motto for many people these days is, "Don't get mad, get a Web page."

—Carey Heckman

While the Internet is in many ways revolutionizing the way we lead our lives, it is a revolution that does not appear to include changing the identity and nature of those in power. Those who think the technology can produce a viable democratic public sphere by itself where policy has failed to do so are deluding themselves.

—Robert McChesney

The Internet as a market can be compared to the Mediterranean Sea. Only if you navigate it with the right ships are you able to reach your new trading partners.

—Walid Mougayar

On the Internet, nobody knows you're a dog.

—One dog to another, in a New Yorker *cartoon*

You can't define news on the Web since everyone with a home page is a global town crier.

—Joshua Quittner

We've all heard that a million monkeys banging on a million typewriters will eventually reproduce the entire works of Shakespeare. Now, thanks to the Internet, we know this is not true.

—Robert Silensky

The glory of the Internet is that it provides global presence, and it's the great equalizer.

—Laurie Tucker

Most of that stuff on the information highway is road kill.

—John Updike

[B]logs have speedily matured into the most vivifying, talent-swapping, socializing breakthrough in popular journalism since the burst of coffeehouse periodicals and political pamphleteering in the 18th century. . . . If Addison and Steele, the editors of *The Spectator* and *The Tatler*, were alive and holding court at Starbucks, they'd be Wi-Fi-ing into a joint blog. If Tom Paine were alive and paroled, he'd be blog-jamming against the Patriot Act, whose very name he'd find obscene.

—*James Wolcott*

See also *Technology and the Media*

Journalism

Journalism is literature in a hurry.

—Matthew Arnold

What is happening today, unfortunately, is that the lowest form of popular culture—lack of information, misinformation, disinformation, and a contempt for the truth or the reality of most people's lives—has overrun real journalism.

—Carl Bernstein

It's all storytelling, you know. That's what journalism is all about.

—Tom Brokaw

Journalism could be described as turning one's enemies into money.

—Craig Brown

Journalism is the only job that requires no degrees, no diplomas and no specialized knowledge of any kind.

—Patrick Campbell

Modern journalism began around 1890 with the advent of a national system of communication and has had a pretty long run. Its time now seems to be about up.

—James Carey, 1996

What would you say if a newspaper reporter, because of his fastidiousness or from a wish to give pleasure to his readers, were to describe only honest mayors, high-minded ladies and virtuous railroad contractors?

—Anton Chekhov

Journalism largely consists in saying "Lord Jones Dead" to people who never knew Lord Jones was alive.

—G. K. Chesterton

Whatever else one may say about the newspaper business, self-examination is one of its virtues. Searching questions about right conduct or wrong conduct are put whenever journalists gather.

—Marquis W. Childs

The First Law of Journalism: to confirm existing prejudice, rather than contradict it.

—Alexander Cockburn

Carelessness is not fatal to journalism, nor are cliches, for the eye rests lightly on them. But what is intended to be read once can seldom be read more than once; a journalist has to accept the fact that his work, by its very todayness, is excluded from any share in tomorrow.

—Cyril Connolly

Literature is the art of writing something that will be read twice; journalism what will be grasped at once.

—Cyril Connolly

Journalism consists in buying white paper at two cents a pound and selling it at ten cents a pound.

—Charles Dana

To the wholesome training of severe newspaper work, when I was a very young man, I constantly refer my first successes.

—Charles Dickens

Newspapers are supposed to explain the community, not convene it. News reporters are supposed to explore the issues, not solve them. Newspapers are supposed to expose the wrongs, not campaign against them. Reporters and city editors are not supposed to write legislation or lead campaigns or pass moral judgments.

—Michael Gartner, on the
"menace" of public journalism

So let us drudge on about our inescapably impossible task of providing every week a first rough draft of a history that will never be completed about a world we can never understand.

—Philip L. Graham

Media is a word that has come to mean bad journalism.

—Graham Greene

Journalism: history on the run.

—Thomas Griffith

The first essence of journalism is to know what you want to know; the second, is to find out who will tell you.

—John Gunther

Journalism allows its readers to witness history.

—John Hersey

Properly practiced, public journalism is simply good journalism without bad habits.

—Ellen Hume

What some in the press regard as investigative journalism seems to many to be simple voyeurism.

—Kathleen Hall Jamieson

The one thing that a good journalist wants is to blend into the background. We should never be the story.

—Peter Jennings

I believe in the profession of journalism. I believe that the public journal is a public trust; that all connected with it are, to the full measure of their responsibility, trustees for the public; that the acceptance of a lesser service is a betrayal of that trust.

—The Journalist's Creed, on a plaque at the
National Press Club in Washington, DC

Today too many newspapers believe in devalued reporting. Worse, newspapers have become the enemy of writing. It began, I think, with the emergence of *USA Today*. . . . Every newspaper in the country has made changes based on what they've seen in *USA Today*. Those changes, I believe, have hurt journalism as a whole. It's all packaging now. It's color graphics and pie charts and news nuggets. I call it Wizard of Oz journalism. No heart, no brain, no courage—and when you look behind the colorful front, there's nothing there. It's empty, a trick, a fraud.

—Dave Kindred

Take the personalities out of our journalism and it would go into bankruptcy.

—Henry King, 1871

All journalism involves some degree of risk, because it is basically an anarchical activity that thrives on exposure, disrespect and creating mischief.

—Phillip Knightley

Mass communication defines the culture, and journalism is more important than ever. Other popular languages, like advertising and public relations, are used for political or commercial persuasion. Journalism is the popular language used in pursuit of truth.

—Joan Konner

An awful lot of [public journalism] is pseudo journalism. If there's a kind of "celebratory tinge" to your journalism, it's easy to overlook things that don't fit into your mold.

—Bill Kovach

Big-time American journalism is group journalism. More than illness or death, the American journalist fears standing alone against the whim of his owners or the prejudice of his audience. Deprive William Safire of the insignia of *The New York Times,* and he would have a hard time selling his truths to a weekly broadsheet in suburban Duluth.

—Lewis H. Lapham

People may expect too much of journalism. Not only do they expect it to be entertaining, they expect it to be true.

—Lewis H. Lapham

Journalism is still an underdeveloped profession and, accordingly, newspapermen are quite often regarded as were surgeons and musicians a century ago, as having the rank, roughly speaking, of barbers and riding masters.

—Walter Lippmann

I don't think it's new that American journalism has found ways to follow the crowd and to find the cheaper end of the carnival side-show with the two-headed woman and the calf that gives birth to a pop singer. That's always been there. What's interesting is that serious journalists are beginning to follow that now.

—Robert MacNeil

Journalism is a license to dabble at the margins of great writing, without the risks.

—*Robert MacNeil*

Journalism is a literary genre very similar to that of the novel, and has the great advantage that the reporter can invent things. And that is completely forbidden to the novelist.

—*Gabriel García Márquez*

Most of the evils of journalism are due to the stupidity, cowardice and Philistinism of working newspapermen.

—*H. L. Mencken*

Public journalism is a response to two 1990s' dilemmas: First, Americans are increasingly withdrawn from public life, cynical about their leaders' ability or interest in doing the right things and at the same time increasingly discouraged about their own ability to affect that woeful situation. And secondly, the fact that journalism is rapidly reaching the last of its supply of credibility and authority with citizens, as is consistently demonstrated by numerous studies and surveys. We believe the two dilemmas are directly connected.

—*Davis "Buzz" Merritt*

It used to be said that journalism is history in a hurry. . . . To cope with the acceleration of social change in today's world, journalism must become social science in a hurry. . . . The ground rules are no different from those on which we've always operated: find the facts, tell what they mean and do it without wasting time. If there are new tools to enable us to perform this task with greater power, accuracy and insight, then we should make the most of them.

—*Philip Meyer*

The day you write to please everyone you no longer are in journalism. You are in show business.

—*Frank Miller Jr.*

Surely the glory of journalism is its transience.

—*Malcolm Muggeridge*

Journalism: A profession whose business it is to explain to others what it personally does not understand.

—*Lord Northcliffe*

. . . always fight for progress and reform, never tolerate injustice and corruption, always fight demagogues of all parties,
never belong to any party, always oppose privileged classes
and public plunderers, never lack sympathy with the poor, always remain devoted to the public welfare, never be satisfied
with merely printing news; always be drastically independent;
never be afraid to attack wrong, whether by predatory plu-
tocracy or predatory poverty.

—*Joseph Pulitzer*

Committing journalism is . . . so important that it's constitu-
tionally protected. We need to think all the time about what
we are doing with that privilege. When we write without that
moral perspective . . . we're like the atheist in his coffin: all
dressed up and no place to go.

—*Jane Bryant Quinn*

A news sense is really a sense of what is important, what is
vital, what has color and life—what people are interested in.
That's journalism.

—*Burton Rascoe*

News is a business. It has always been. Journalists understand
and accept that. But journalism is something else too. Something more. It is a light on the horizon. A beacon that helps

the citizens of a democracy find their way. News is an essential component of a free society. News is a business but it is also a public trust.

—*Dan Rather*

Every good journalist is at least vaguely aware that his trade may one day go the way of phrenology—and, what's more, the population will hardly protest the extinction.

—*David Remnick*

I believe in public journalism, too . . . but my definition involves covering public meetings, not sponsoring them.

—*Gene Roberts*

While journalists treasure their role as watchdog and critic, increasingly they are seen as insiders themselves, part of a discredited political class.

—*Jay Rosen*

Dear Sir: Your profession has, as usual, destroyed your brain.

—*George Bernard Shaw, writing to a journalist*

Cynicism, not liberalism, is the guiding force throughout much of American journalism.

—*Ed Siegel*

I share the concerns that have been raised about the downsides of the press, and I think we are sensationalistic and lousy at times. But I also worry that our fault at times is that we're too timid in journalism. Often our problem is not that we are too aggressive, but that we don't go after the powerful with the best of intentions and the best in journalism in the way we should, and we don't give voice to the voiceless in the way that our papers and our electronic journalism should in covering the important issues of our times.

—*Robert M. Steele*

All newspaper and journalistic activity is an intellectual brothel from which there is no retreat.

—*Leo Tolstoy*

The only qualities essential for real success in journalism are ratlike cunning, a plausible manner and a little literary ability. The capacity to steal other people's ideas and phrases . . . is also invaluable.

—*Nicolas Tomalin*

Journalism is the ability to meet the challenge of filling space.

—*Rebecca West*

The overwhelming conclusion I have drawn from my life in journalism—nearly thirty years so far . . . —is that the American press, powerful as it unquestionably is and protected though it may be by the Constitution and the laws, is not often "robust and uninhibited" but is usually timid and anxious—for respectability at least as much as for profitability.

—*Tom Wicker*

The difference between journalism and literature is that journalism is unreadable and literature is not read.

—*Oscar Wilde*

Journalism: organized gossip.

—*Oscar Wilde*

The public have an insatiable curiosity to know everything. Except what is worth knowing. Journalism, conscious of this, and having tradesman-like habits, supplies their demands.

—*Oscar Wilde*

What's facing print journalism is a failure of confidence.

—*William Woo*

What has exploded is not news, but talk about news; commentary, not information . . . It's cocktail-party chat passing for journalism.

—*Richard Zoglin*

See also *Journalists; Reporters*

Journalists

[Journalists] are a sort of assassins who sit with loaded blunderbusses at the corner of streets and fire them off for sport at any passenger they select.

—John Quincy Adams

Of one trait journalists have rarely been accused: that of humility. If they are ever to develop a clear understanding of what they do, and how what they do fits into the social order around them, it will be necessary for them to surrender their arrogance . . .

—J. Herbert Altschull

With all that can be said, justly, against journalists, there is one kind of journalist to whom civilization owes a very great debt, namely, the brave and honest reporter who unearths and makes public unpleasant facts, cases of injustice, cruelty, corruption, which the authorities would like to keep hidden, and which even the average reader would prefer not to be compelled to think about.

—W. H. Auden

No news is good news; no journalists is even better.

—Nicolas Bentley

The smarter the journalists are, the better off society is. [For] to a degree, people read the press to inform themselves—and the better the teacher, the better the student body.

—*Warren Buffet*

Too much of what you write on many of these beats is written for the approval of your fellow participants in the game, for your editors to some degree, and hardly at all for the comprehension and approval of a wider public, most of which you tend to think of with the same contempt as government officials.

—*Hodding Carter*

Journalists have always been our most old-fashioned class, being too busy with the news of the day to lay aside the mental habits of fifty years before.

—*Frank Moore Colby*

Three centuries after the birth of the first American newspaper, the public is still deciding what kind of journalist it wants and what kind of freedom it will grant that journalist.

—*Loren Ghiglione*

A news-writer is a man without virtue, who writes lies at home for his own profit. To these compositions is required neither genius nor knowledge, neither industry nor sprightliness; but contempt of shame and indifference to truth are absolutely necessary.

—*Samuel Johnson*

If I were a father and had a daughter who was seduced, I would not despair over her. But if I had a son who became a journalist and continued to remain one for five years, I would give him up.

—*Sören Kierkegaard*

Whenever you find hundreds of thousands of sane people trying to get out of a place and a little bunch of madmen struggling to get in, you know the latter are newspapermen.

—*H. R. Knickerbocker*

A journalist is stimulated by a deadline; he writes worst when he has time.

—*Karl Kraus*

To have no thoughts and be able to express them—that's what makes a journalist.

—*Karl Kraus*

Biting journalists should allow no hand to feed them.

—*Sinclair Lewis, declining a U.S. government invitation to visit and report on a foreign country*

The pattern of a newspaperman's life is like the plot of Black Beauty. Sometimes he finds a kind master who gives him a dry stall and an occasional bran mash in the form of a Christmas bonus; sometimes he falls into the hands of a mean owner who drives him in spite of spavins and expects him to live on banana peelings.

—*A. J. Liebling*

A good journalist will find news rather than a hack. If he sees a building with a dangerous list, he does not have to wait until it falls into the street in order to recognize news.

—*Walter Lippmann*

More newspapermen have been ruined by self-importance than by liquor.

—*Walter Lippmann*

I became a journalist to come as close as possible to the heart of the world.

—*Henry R. Luce*

[To be a journalist you need] vision, technical competence and passion, all in equal measure. . . . If you have just vision and passion, you're a dreamer. If you have just technical competence and passion, you're a bureaucrat. You need all three.

—Nancy Hicks Maynard

There are honest journalists like there are honest politicians. When bought they stay bought.

—Bill Moyers, building on Will Rogers'
definition of an honest politician

A journalist is a grumbler, a censurer, a giver of advice, a regent of sovereigns, a tutor of nations. Four hostile journalists are more to be feared than a thousand bayonets.

—Napoleon

Reporters, once identified most closely with ordinary people, now more often than not are elites. . . . [They] have "abandoned the old neighborhood" and have gone uptown, losing touch with many or most readers.

—Al Neuharth

Doctors bury their mistakes; lawyers send theirs to jail. Only journalists sign their mistakes and print them on the front page.

—Newsroom adage

Auditors always reject any newsman's expense account with a bottom line divisible by 5 or 10.

—Emmet N. O'Brien

As newsmen became imbued with a sense of responsibility, they contended that the public had a right of access to information, had a basic right to be informed, and that the press was the agent of the public in breaking down barriers to the free flow of news.

—Theodore Peterson

Journalists belong in the gutter because that is where the ruling classes throw their dirty secrets.

—Gerald Priestland

Scratch a journalist and you find a reformer.

—Leo Rosten

White journalists and non-white journalists are light years apart in their perceptions. . . . Dialogue, however difficult or politically incorrect, is the only way to start fixing it.

—Gerald M. Sass

A journalist is a man who has missed his calling.

—Otto von Bismarck (attributed)

The journalist belongs to a sort of pariah caste.

—Max Weber

You cannot hope to bribe or twist,
Thank God, the British journalist;
But seeing what the man will do
Unbribed, there's no occasion to.

—Humbert Wolfe

A statesman is an easy man,
He tells his lies by rote;
A journalist makes up his lies
And takes you by the throat;
So stay at home and drink your beer
And let the neighbors vote.

—William Butler Yeats

See also *First Amendment; Journalism; Reporters; Sources and Subjects*

Language and Words

Words are all we have.

—Samuel Beckett

People endowed with a gift of words out of proportion to their native intelligence, no matter how much improved by training and learning—such people can become a public danger, socially, politically, and above all culturally.

—Bernard Berenson

Language is magic: it makes things appear and disappear.

—Nicole Brossard

Words are like money; there is nothing so useless, unless when in actual use.

—Samuel Butler

The words! I collected them in all shapes and sizes, and hung them like bangles in my mind.

—Hortense Calisher

Alice had not the slightest idea what latitude was, or longitude either, but she thought they were nice grand words to say.

—Lewis Carroll

"When *I* use a word," Humpty Dumpty said, in rather a scornful tone, "it means just what I choose it to mean—neither more nor less."

"The question is," said Alice, "whether you *can* make words mean so many different things."

"The question is," said Humpty Dumpty, "which is to be master—that's all."

—Lewis Carroll

Words are the dress of thoughts, which should no more be presented in rags, tatters and dirt than your person should.

—Lord Chesterfield

The beginning of a wise policy is to call things by their right name.

—Chinese proverb

Broadly speaking, the short words are the best, and the old words best of all.

—Winston Churchill

In language, clearness is everything.

—Confucius

With words we govern men.

—Benjamin Disraeli

You can stroke people with words.

—F. Scott Fitzgerald

Good words cost no more than bad.

—Thomas Fuller

Simple, short sentences don't always work.

—Theodore Geisel (Dr. Seuss)

Like a diaphanous nightgown, language both hides and reveals.
—*Karen Elizabeth Gordon*

Words are really a mask. They rarely express the true meaning; in fact, they tend to hide it.
—*Herman Hesse*

Never impose your language on people you wish to reach.
—*Abbie Hoffman*

Language is by its very nature a communal thing; that is, it expresses never the exact thing but a compromise—that which is common to you, me, and everybody.
—*Thomas Earnest Hulme*

The function of language is twofold: to communicate emotion and to give information.
—*Aldous Huxley*

Thanks to words, we have been able to rise above the brutes; and thanks to words, we have often sunk to the level of the demons.
—*Aldous Huxley*

Well-chosen phrases are a great help in the smuggling of offensive ideas.
—*Vladimir Jabotinsky*

Words, like eyeglasses, blur everything that they do not make clear.
—*Joseph Joubert*

Some words are like the old Roman galleys; large-scaled and ponderous. They sit low in the water even when their cargo is light.
—*William Jovanovich*

Words are, of course, the most powerful drug used by mankind.

—*Rudyard Kipling*

Next in criminality to him who violates the laws of his country is he who violates the language.

—*Walter Savage Landor*

Buffaloes are held by cords, man by his words.

—*Malay proverb*

When an age is in the throes of profound transition, the first thing to disintegrate is language.

—*Rollo May*

He respects Owl, because you can't help respecting anybody who can spell Tuesday, even if he doesn't spell it right.

—*A. A. Milne*

Many of the world's misunderstandings are caused by grammar.

—*Montaigne*

The word is half his that speaks, and half his that hears it.

—*Montaigne*

The present age shrinks from precision and "understands" only soft woolly words which really have no particular meaning, like "cultural heritage" or "the exigent dictates of modern traffic needs."

—*Flann O'Brien*

Language makes culture, and we make a rotten culture when we abuse words.

—*Cynthia Ozick*

Clearness is the most important matter in the use of words.

—*Quintillian*

Words not only affect us temporarily; they change us, they socialize or unsocialize us.

—David Reisman

Words are the wings of action.

—Jean Paul Richter

I'm allergic to spelling.

—Barney Saltzberg, Phoebe and the Spelling Bee

The difference between the right word and the almost right word is the difference between lightning and the lightning bug.

—Mark Twain

I never write "metropolis" for seven cents when I can get the same price for "city."

—Mark Twain

One can seldom run his pen through an adjective without improving his manuscript.

—Mark Twain

We dissect nature along lines laid down by our native language. . . . Language is not simply a reporting device for experience but a defining framework for it.

—Benjamin Lee Whorf

See also *Writers and Writing*

Law

The constitutional guarantees require, we think, a federal rule that prohibits a public official from recovering damages for a defamatory falsehood relating to his official conduct unless he proves that the statement was made with "actual malice"— that is, with knowledge that it was false or with reckless disregard of whether it was false or not.

—William Brennan

Only the first and second prongs of the Miller test—appeal to prurient interest and patent offensiveness—should be decided with reference to "contemporary community standards." The ideas that a work represents need not obtain majority approval to merit protection, and the value of that work does not vary from community to community based on the degree of local acceptance it has won. The proper inquiry is not whether an ordinary member of any given community would find serious value in the allegedly obscene material, but whether a reasonable person would find such value in the material as a whole.

—Warren E. Burger

Time, place and circumstances determine the constitutional protection of utterance.

—William O. Douglas

The right of free speech does not include, however, the right to use the facilities of radio without a license. The licensing

110

system established by Congress in the Communications Act of 1934 was a proper exercise of its power over commerce. The standard it provided for the licensing of stations was the "public interest, convenience, or necessity." Denial of a station license on that ground, if valid under the Act, is not a denial of free speech.

—Felix Frankfurter

Perhaps it could be said that, with few exceptions, only lawyers win libel suits.

—Don Gillmor

My own motto is publish and be sued.

—Richard Ingrams

Evidence is not evidence until it comes from [the courtroom], not the 11 o'clock news.

—Lance Ito, judge in the O. J. Simpson trial

States which do not allow truth as a defense to protect printers from libel or other prosecutions go too far in restraining a free press. Libel damages should only apply to personal defamations.

—Thomas Jefferson

The absence of seditious libel as a crime is the true pragmatic test of freedom of speech.

—Harry Kalven Jr.

The Net has created a new kind of First Amendment that is, in many ways, more vivid and powerful than the non-virtual one.

—Jon Katz

It's troubling that whenever a new technology [is introduced] . . . the reaction is to throw the First, Fourth, Fourteenth and whatever other amendments you choose out the window.

—Jane Kirtley

The greater the truth, the greater the libel.

—*Legal maxim, colonial era*

I wish I could sue *The New York Post* but it's awfully hard to sue a garbage can.

—*Paul Newman*

Newspapers are conducted by men who are laymen to the law. With too rare exceptions their capacity for misunderstanding the significance of legal events and procedures, not to speak of opinions, is great. But this is neither remarkable nor peculiar to newsmen. For the law, as lawyers best know, is full of perplexities.

—*John Rutledge*

If the rash of lawsuits [for libel and invasion of privacy] makes us more careful, more compassionate and more sensitive to people and their needs, they may not be all bad. But if they keep us from being aggressive and fulfilling our responsibilities to our readers, to our communities and our country, they will remove one of the major checks in our Constitution's marvelous set of checks and balances.

—*Thomas Schumaker*

Who steals my purse steals trash; 'tis something, nothing.
'Twas mine, 'tis his, and has been slave to thousands;
But he that filches from me my good name
Robs me of that which not enriches him
And makes me poor indeed.

—*William Shakespeare,* Othello

Intellectual-property laws have given [the United States] the edge in technology—and ironically, allowed us to have programs like Napster. Without [these laws], we wouldn't be the tech capital of the world. In the 16th century, for instance, the Spanish empire didn't protect ship designers, so they all moved to England, and then England turned around and kicked Spain's butt in some big, important war. England is still a big, important country. Have you ever even heard of Spain?

—*Joel Stein*

This dynamic, multifaceted category of communications includes not only traditional print and news services, but also audio, video, and still images, as well as interactive, real-time dialogue. . . . As the District Court found, "the content on the Internet is as diverse as human thought." We agree with its conclusion that our cases provide no basis for qualifying the level of First Amendment scrutiny that should be applied to this medium.

—*John Paul Stevens*

There are laws to protect the freedom of the press's speech, but none that are worth anything to protect the people from the press.

—*Mark Twain*

How much license does the press have to destroy people's reputations?

—*Coleman Young*

See also *The First Amendment*

Magazines

Magazine: A large pamphlet issued at regular intervals, usually bulging with coupons. Used to cover coffee tables.

—Anonymous

This is the age of Magazines
    Even skeptics must confess it:
Where is the town of much renown
    That has not one to bless it?

—Anonymous, 1824, on the proliferation
of magazines in the United States

A magazine: Five pounds of advertisements mixed with fiction.

—Cynic's Cyclopaedia

Backward ran sentences until reeled the mind.

—Wolcott Gibbs, parodying the
early style of Time *magazine*

There is hardly any subject or part of a subject that does not have a magazine. What used to be considered specialized publications—sports and music, for example—have given way to specific sports (e.g., paddle sports) and specific music (e.g., rap) titles. They are taking the lead in this new age of ultra-specialized publications.

—Samir A. Husni

Editing a magazine is not a good way to make friends.

> —*William Kristol, editor and publisher*
> *of* The Weekly Standard

Magazines all too frequently lead to books and should be regarded as the heavy petting of literature.

> —*Fran Lebowitz*

A *Time* story must be completely organized from beginning to end; it must go from nowhere to somewhere and sit down when it arrives.

> —*Henry R. Luce, founder of* Time

I am a Protestant and a free enterpriser, which means I am biased in favor of God, Eisenhower and the stockholders of Time Inc., and if anyone who objects doesn't know this by now, why the hell are they still spending 35 cents for the magazine?

> —*Henry R. Luce*

If mass magazines thought they could attract millions of readers [in the 1950s] by appealing to mass taste, they were hopelessly outmatched by television's ability to do the same.

> —*Therese Lueck*

The magazine in the end will be the most influential of all departments of letters.

> —*Edgar Allen Poe*

Of all the literary scenes
Saddest this sight to me:
The graves of little magazines
Who died to make verse free.

> —*Keith Preston*

You can't ask people what they want and, based on those comments, concoct a magazine, for the simple reason that people only know what they want after you've delivered it to them.

—Joaquim Preuss, Der Spiegel

The New Yorker will not be edited for the old lady from Dubuque.

—Harold Ross

In magazines that accept cigarette advertising I was unable to find a single article, in several years of publication, that would have given readers any clear notion of the nature and extent of the medical and social havoc wreaked by the cigarette-smoking habit.

—R. C. Smith, based on studying seven years' content
after cigarette ads were banned on TV

Young is better than old, pretty is better than ugly, television is better than music, music is better than movies, movies are better than sports, and anything is better than politics . . . but nothing is better than a dead celebrity.

—Richard B. Stolley, on People *magazine's covers*

I simply hunt for things that interest me, and if they do, I print them.

—DeWitt Wallace, founder of Reader's Digest

All "little" magazines have the luxury of thinking the reader is the same person as their editors.

—William Whitworth, editor, Atlantic Monthly

There is only one comfortable place for a mass magazine to be—first.

—James Playsted Wood

Miscellaneous

In the United States today we have more than our fair share of the nattering nabobs of negativism. They have formed their own Four H Club—the hopeless, hysterical, hypochondriacs of history.

—Spiro Agnew

Print is the doctor who actually looks at the thermometer and sees what the President's temperature is, and television is the public address system that broadcasts it all over the hospital.

—Jonathan Alter

Movies and TV are the center of our culture, alas.

—Alfred Appel

What the mass media offer is not popular art, but entertainment which is intended to be consumed like food, forgotten, and replaced by a new dish.

—W. H. Auden

The splendor of an editor's speech and the splendor of his newspaper are inversely related to the distance between the city in which he makes his speech and the city in which he publishes his newspaper.

—Ben H. Bagdikian

All this programming diversity and special-interest narrow-casting replaces communication with group narcissism. The tube now becomes a mirror showing us only ourselves, relentlessly screening out any images that do not suit our own special prejudices and group norms. . . . Every parochial voice gets a hearing (though only before the already converted), and the public as a whole is left with no voice. No global village, but a Tower of Babel: a hundred chattering mouths bereft of any common language.

—Benjamin Barber

The truth is, print still matters most. TV is entirely derivative. They wouldn't know what to do if they couldn't read *The New York Times* and *The Washington Post*, or *The New Republic* and *The Weekly Standard*.

—Fred Barnes

We have this fantasy that if we just have enough information, we can control events.

—Barbara Biesecker

Television is good at the transmission of experience. Print is better at the transmission of facts.

—John Chancellor

The media serve the interests of the state and corporate power . . . [and] not only allow the agendas of news to be bent in accordance with state demands and criteria of utility, they also accept the presuppositions of the state without question.

—Noam Chomsky

Today our society needs, first, a truthful, comprehensive, and intelligent account of the day's events in a context which gives them meaning; second, a forum for the exchange of comment and criticism; third, a means of projecting the opinions and attitudes of the groups in the society to one another; fourth, a method of presenting and clarifying the goals and values of the society; and, fifth, a way of reaching every member of the society by the currents of information, thought, and feeling which the press supplies.

Commission on Freedom of the Press, 1947

The American media produce a product of very poor quality. Its information is not reliable; it has too much chrome and glitz; its doors rattle; it breaks down almost immediately; and it's sold without warranty. It's flash but it's basically junk.

—*Michael Crichton*

Over 50 years' experience of the mass media—press, film, radio, television—have conditioned us, both at the national and international levels, to a single kind of information flow, which we have come to accept as normal and indeed as the only possible kind: a vertical, one-way flow from the top downwards of non-diversified anonymous messages, produced by a few and addressed to all. This is not communication.

—*Jean d'Arcy*

Where is the wisdom we have lost in knowledge? Where is the knowledge we have lost in information?

—*T. S. Eliot*

The proliferation of channels of information and news outlets doesn't mean we're better informed. We're just ill-informed about more things.

—*Jim Gaines*

We're in the realm of science fiction now. Whoever controls the media—the images—controls the culture.

—*Allen Ginsberg*

Those who fight profit-making corporations promote their own anticorporate logos. Greenpeace has its own, as do campaigners against capitalist globalization. Critics may try to make the media torrent swerve, but cannot imagine drying it up. In the country of the branded, even the opponents brand themselves.

—Todd Gitlin

The 24-hour media are often all dressed up with nowhere to go.

—Jennifer Harper

Everywhere I go, kids walk around not with books in their arms, but with radios to their heads. Children can't read or write, but they can memorize whole albums.

—Jesse Jackson

The last thing media people can do is to come alive to the historical processes in which they are inextricably caught up and adapt their styles and priorities within them. Theirs has always been and will continue to be only a supportive role—supportive of values and systems that are not theirs to prescribe. Those values and systems are fashioned by economic and social forces much larger and more fundamental than themselves. The media ego must learn to diminish gracefully.

—Neville Jayaweera

[M]edia culture is so deeply imbued with a typically post-modern sense that the only absolute truth is that there are no absolute truths or that, if there were, they would be inaccessible to human reason and therefore irrelevant. In such a view, what matters is not the truth but "the story" . . .

—Pope John Paul II

We may already have reached the point in this country where the media, our greatest check on other accumulations of power, may themselves be beyond the reach of any other institutions.

—Nicholas Johnson

The role of the press in developing countries is also to provide hope. By excessive criticism we might be self-defeating.

—Aristides Katoppo

Along with the country as a whole, the press has too long basked in a white world, looking out of it, if at all, with white men's eyes and a white perspective. That is no longer good enough.

—Kerner Commission on Civil Disorders, 1968

The media are sheep in wolves' clothing. They look tough, but they're followers.

—Jeffrey Klein

Can one really distinguish between the mass media as instruments of information and entertainment, and as agents of manipulation and indoctrination?

—Herbert Marcuse

What you *see* is news, what you *know* is background, what you *feel* is opinion.

—Lester Markel

Our capacity to communicate is beginning to totally overwhelm our ability to communicate with each other.

—Nancy Hicks Maynard

The medium is the message.

—Marshall McLuhan

Probably half of them, indeed, are simply refuges for students too stupid to tackle the other professions.

—H. L. Mencken, on journalism schools

The media are always looking for a problem.

—Mary Lee Merrill

We are drowning in information but starved for knowledge.

—John Naisbett

When you run a picture of a nice clean-cut all American girl like this, get her tits above the fold.

—Al Neuharth (attributed)

Never lose your sense of the superficial.

—Lord Northcliffe

In recent years, both print and broadcast journalism have been the subject of a growing if irrational suspicion—sometimes expressed in high places—that the press is somehow to blame for unhappy events and trends merely because it performs its duty of reporting them.

—William S. Paley

What [the media] do is to affect the *acoustics* of society, the lighting, the way we see and hear things. They act as resonators, amplifiers, public address systems, spotlights. But in themselves they are sterile and empty. They are bridges waiting for somebody to cross them, mirrors waiting for something to reflect, and those who make their living in them are constantly waiting about for something or somebody to make use of them.

—Gerald Priestland

The larger trends we see in the data on content, audience, economics, ownership and newsroom investment all could add to public distrust of the new media. There is something, in other words, of a vicious cycle in the public attitude data. As declining audience leads to newsroom cutbacks and other financial fixes, these reinforce the public's suspicions that news organizations are motivated more by economics than public service.

—The Project for Excellence in Journalism

A professorship of journalism is as absurd as a professorship of matrimony.

*—Joseph Pulitzer (an early criticism;
he later strongly supported journalism education)*

Yelling about the media is like bellowing at the umpire. Maybe it can't change the calls reporters and editors made about yesterday's story, but it might make a difference in tomorrow's.

—Eleanor Randolph

You can be a black or you can be a journalist. Being a reporter pays a lot better than being a nigger.

—William Raspberry, African-American columnist

The infotainment often appeals to audiences that give little, if any, attention to more serious media. In that respect, those that contain even minimal amounts of information *can* help these people make decisions—they can help make democracy work.

—Carol Reuss

[The word] media is the plural for mediocre.

—Rene Saguisag

I have been appalled to watch "the press" metamorphose into "the news media" and, ultimately, into "the media," occupying a small corner of a vast entertainment stage.

—Daniel Schorr

Today a major break with the past is clearly at hand, and with it will come . . . an important shift in the way we treat information, the way we collect and store it, the way we classify, censor and circulate it.

—Anthony Smith

Everybody gets so much information all day long that they lose their common sense.

—Gertrude Stein

After 200 years of fixed tradition and accepted practice, American journalists are now facing a new situation: If knowledge is power, it is no longer concentrated in the hands of the powerful. . . . By shaping our picture of the world on an almost minute-to-minute basis, the media now largely determine what we think, how we feel and what we do about our social and political environment.

—*Robert Stein*

The media. It sounds like a convention of spiritualists.

—*Tom Stoppard,* Night and Day

If we had had the technology back then, you would have seen Eva Braun on the "Donahue" show and Hitler on "Meet the Press."

—*Ed Turner*

There are only two forces that can carry light to all corners of the globe—the sun in the heavens and the Associated Press.

—*Mark Twain*

In the future everybody will be world famous for fifteen minutes.

—*Andy Warhol*

Most rock journalism is people who can't write interviewing people who can't talk for people who can't read.

—*Frank Zappa*

See also *The Press*

Mottos and Slogans

If you don't want it printed, don't let it happen.
>—Aspen Daily News

Covers Dixie like the dew.
>—The Atlanta Journal

Light for all.
>—The Baltimore Sun

A relatively independent newspaper.
>—The Bettendorf News, *Iowa*

Help America discover Columbus
>—The Columbus Daily Advocate, *Columbus, Kan.*

Our aim: to fear God, tell the truth and make money.
>—Daily Herald, *Arlington Heights, Illinois*

The only newspaper in the world that gives a damn about Jacksonville, NC.
>—The Jacksonville Daily News

Not for love, honor or fame, but for cash.
>—The Marble Hill Era, *Indiana*

Enquiring minds want to know.

—The National Enquirer

It shines for ALL.

—The New York Sun

All the news that's fit to print.

—The New York Times

Let there be light and people will find their own way.

—*The Scripps Howard Newspaper Group*

Movies

A continuous clash of egomaniacal monsters, wasting more energy than dinosaurs and pouring rivers of money into the sand.

—Robert Bolt, on the movie industry

Anybody can direct. There are only eleven good writers.

—Mel Brooks

The most expensive art form ever invented.

—Mel Brooks

Nothing would disgust me more morally than winning an Oscar.

—Luis Buñuel

The British Film Industry is alive and well and living in Los Angeles.

—Michael Caine

Through the magic of motion pictures, someone who's never left Peoria knows the softness of Paris spring, the color of the Nile sunset, the sorts of vegetables one will find along the upper Amazon and that Big Ben has not yet gone digital.

—Vincent Canby

There are no rules in filmmaking. Only sins. And the cardinal sin is dullness.

—Frank Capra

The cinema is little more than a fad. It's canned drama. What audiences really want to see is flesh and blood on the stage.
—*Charlie Chaplin, ca. 1916*

A film is a petrified fountain of thought.
—*Jean Cocteau*

A film set is a never-ending hell.
—*Tom Conti*

Gone with the Wind is going to be the biggest flop in Hollywood history. I'm just glad it'll be Clark Gable who's falling flat on his face, and not Gary Cooper.
—*Gary Cooper*

The new literature.
—*Cecil B. DeMille*

Girls bore me—they still do. I love Mickey Mouse more than any woman I've ever known.
—*Walt Disney*

[Criticism of Hollywood] is not a crusade for censorship but a call for good citizenship.
—*Robert Dole*

Cinema: A refuge for those who are weary of life.
—*Georges Duhamel*

"Make my day" came from the screenwriter Joe Stinson. Only thing I did, I reprised it at the end—that's my contribution. I saw the line as a goodie.
—*Clint Eastwood*

Movies are fun. But they're not a cure for cancer.
—*Clint Eastwood*

Hollywood is a place where your best friend will plunge a knife in your back and then call the police to tell them that you are carrying a concealed weapon.

—George Frazier

"Movies should have a beginning, a middle and an end," harrumphed French film maker Georges Franju. . . . "Certainly," replied Jean-Luc Godard. "But not necessarily in that order."

—Jean-Luc Godard

A wide screen just makes a bad film twice as bad.

—Sam Goldwyn

If you want to send a message, call Western Union.

—Sam Goldwyn, on the lack of
seriousness in Hollywood movies

The length of a film should be directly related to the endurance of the human bladder.

—Alfred Hitchcock

All television did was shrink the demand for ordinary movies. The demand for extraordinary movies increased. If any one thing is wrong with the movie industry today, it is the unrelenting effort to astonish.

—Clive James

The cinema, like the detective story, makes it possible to experience without danger all the excitement, passion and desire which must be repressed in a humanitarian ordering of life.

—Carl Jung

Good movies make you care, make you believe in possibilities again.

—Pauline Kael

The words "Kiss Kiss Bang Bang," which I saw on an Italian movie poster, are perhaps the briefest statement imaginable of the basic appeal of movies. This appeal is what attracts us, and ultimately what makes us despair when we begin to understand how seldom movies are more than this.

—Pauline Kael

I hardly think putting some sort of limit on excessive violence in film is a threat to the First Amendment.

—Michael Keaton

. . . a series of catastrophes, ended by a fashion show.

—Oscar Levant, on early newsreels

Strip away the phony tinsel of Hollywood and you find the real tinsel underneath.

—Oscar Levant

My invention . . . can be exploited for a certain time as a scientific curiosity, but apart from that it has no commercial value whatsoever.

—Auguste Lumière, 1895 (French co-inventor of a motion picture camera bearing his name)

Our movies come from our hearts—our little movies, not the Hollywood movies. Our movies are like extensions of our own pulse, of our heartbeat, of our eyes, our fingertips; they are so personal, so unambitious in their movement, in their use of light, their imagery. We want to surround this earth with our film frames and warm it up—until it begins to move.

—Jonas Mekas

Adding sound to movies would be like putting lipstick on the Venus de Milo.

—Mary Pickford, 1925

The medium is too powerful and important an influence on the way we live—the way we see ourselves—to be left solely to the tyranny of the box-office or reduced to the sum of the lowest common denominator of public taste.

—*David Puttnam*

The intensity of movie publicity is in inverse ratio to the quality of the movie.

—*Gene Shalit*

In this business we make movies. American movies. Leave the films to the French.

—*Sam Shephard*

If I could control the medium of the American motion picture, I would need nothing else in order to convert the entire world to Communism.

—*Joseph Stalin*

To express ourselves in good films, we also have to put up with the crap and violence and stupidity of films that are put out by guys who are pure exploiters.

—*Sylvester Stallone*

Reagan doesn't have the presidential look.

—*United Artists casting executive, 1964*

In a free society, no one can command "only good movies be produced."

—*Jack Valenti*

All Americans born between 1890 and 1945 wanted to be movie stars.

—*Gore Vidal*

Who the hell wants to hear actors talk?

—*Harry Warner, of Warner Bros. Studios, ca. 1927*

A director must be a policeman, a midwife, a psychoanalyst, a sycophant and a bastard.

—*Billy Wilder*

A team effort is a lot of people doing what I say.
—*Michael Winner, British film director*

For me, movies should be visual. If you want dialogue, you should read a book.

—*Vilmos Zsigmond, cinematographer*

News

It is an ill office to be the first to herald ill.

—Aeschylus

A dogfight in Brooklyn is bigger than a revolution in China.

—Anonymous, on the importance of local news

The word explains itself, without the muse,
And the four letters speak from whence comes *news*.
From North, East, West, South, the solution's made,
Each quarter gives accounts of war and trade.

—Anonymous

Generally speaking, the press lives on disaster.

—Clement Attlee

Lady Middleton . . . exerted herself to ask Mr. Palmer if there was any news in the paper. "No, none at all," he replied, and read on.

—Jane Austen, Sense and Sensibility

The news is never the whole truth.

—Denis Beckett

I tell the honest truth in my paper and I leave the consequences to God. Could I leave them in better hands?

—James Gordon Bennett Sr.

Harmony seldom makes a headline.

—Silas Bent

We teach our viewers that the trivial is significant, that the lurid and the loopy are more significant than real news.

—Carl Bernstein

Like cold water to a weary soul is good news from a distant land.

—The Bible (Proverbs 25:25)

There is nothing new under the sun.

—The Bible (Ecclesiastes 1:9)

All I have to do to get a story on the front page of every one of the AP's 2,000 clients is to mention in the lead a treatment for piles, ulcers, or sexual impotence—three conditions that every telegraph editor has, or is worried about.

—Alton Blakeslee

When a dog bites a man that is not news, but when a man bites a dog that is news.

—John B. Bogart (also attributed to Charles Dana)

News is what I say it is.

—David Brinkley

Remember that all news is biased.

—H. Jackson Brown Jr.

Everywhere I go I get the "you don't report the good news" stuff. Now I say I know only one paper that prints only good news about its country: Pravda.

—David Burgin

News: What one's colleagues have defined as news.

—Douglass Cater

It's not the world that's got so much worse but the news coverage that's got so much better.

—G. K. Chesterton

News is almost by definition bad news.

—Marquis Childs

What is reported, then, becomes news; it takes on a new quality. . . . In this sense, news takes on a kind of objective reality: what was reported is news; what was not reported—for whatever reasons—is not news. And once it *is* news, it exercises a powerful claim on the attention of reporters.

—Bernard Cohen

Be interesting. Get the news.

—Charles Dana

Whatever Divine Providence permits to occur I am not too proud to report.

—Charles Dana

Nothing is news until it has appeared in *The Times*.

—Ralph Deakin, foreign editor of The Times, *London*

In this age of globalisation, news is much more parochial than in the days when communications from abroad ticked slowly across the world by telegraph. And here is another [paradox]: that in this information age, newspapers which used to be full of politics and economics are thick with stars and sport.

—The Economist

Ill news comes too soon.

—English proverb

No news is good news.

—English proverb

This business of giving people what they want is a dope pusher's argument. News is something people don't know they're interested in until they hear about it. The job of a journalist is to take what's important and make it interesting.

—*Reuven Frank*

I gather all the information I can. I cross out what I don't believe. And I write up the rest. And that's news.

—*Thomas L. Friedman*

For a constituency being conditioned by trashy crime pamphlets, gory novels and overwrought melodramas, news was simply the most exciting, most entertaining content a paper could offer, especially when it was skewed, as it invariably was in the penny press, to the most sensational stories. In fact, one might even say that the masters of the penny press *invented* the concept of news because it was the best way to sell their papers in an entertainment environment.

—*Neal Gabler, on the Penny Press in the 1830s*

Surprise, the stuff news is made of.

—*William E. Giles*

The news is a superficial view of the history of the preceding day. Newsmen cannot do as much research as historians in their studies; but, within limits allowed them by time, geography, censors and deadlines, they try to give the public a slice of history.

—*Philip Gillon*

The difference between news and entertainment is that news requires a judgment of what is significant, while entertainment [requires] a judgment about what people will enjoy.

—*Richard N. Goodwin*

Evil report carries farther than any applause.

—Baltasar Gracian

There is no proposition, no matter how foolish, for which a dozen Nobel signatures cannot be collected. Furthermore, any such petition is guaranteed page-one treatment in *The New York Times*.

—Daniel S. Greenberg

To withhold news is to play God.

—John Loft Hess

We [journalists] are not in the business of helping people feel better about themselves, I'm afraid, because that's called propaganda, not news.

—John Humphreys

He knocks boldly who brings good news.

—Italian proverb

While news is important, news interpretation is far more important.

—H. V. Kaltenborn

A people without reliable news is, sooner or later, a people without the basis of freedom.

—Harold J. Laski

People everywhere confuse what they read in newspapers with news.

—A. J. Liebling

News: What protrudes from the ordinary.

—Walter Lippmann

Bad news drives good news out of the media.

—Lee Loevinger

We welcome almost any break in the monotony of things, and a man has only to murder a series of wives in a new way to become known to millions of people who have never heard of Homer.

—*Robert Lynd*

News is anything that makes a reader say, "Gee whiz!". . . News is whatever a good editor chooses to print.

—*Arthur MacEwen*

Never awake me when you have good news to announce, because with good news nothing presses; but when you have bad news, arouse me immediately, for then there is not an instant to be lost.

—*Napoleon*

News: What somebody wants to suppress. All the rest is advertising.

—*Lord Northcliffe*

A little public scandal is good once in a while—takes the tension out of the news.

—*Beryl Pfizer*

The peculiar value of news is in the spreading of it while it is fresh.

—*Mahlon Pitney*

Literature is news that *stays* news.

—*Ezra Pound*

Bad news does not improve with age.

—*Jody Powell*

Until recently, the point of news wasn't mass narcissism: You didn't read a smoke signal or pick up a Civil War-era magazine or tune in to a radio report on the Normandy landing in order to learn more about yourself. News was stories of *other* people, of the world beyond the self.

—*William Powers*

In many parts of the news media, we are increasingly getting the raw elements of news as the end product. This is particularly true in the newer, 24-hour media. In cable and online, there is a tendency toward a jumbled, chaotic, partial quality in some reports, without much synthesis or even the ordering of information.

—*The Project for Excellence in Journalism*

[Weather] is the only kind of news we can all share in—no matter what our race, class, gender, or political differences— as members of a common community.

—*Elayne Rapping*

The conflict between the men who make and the men who report the news is as old as time. News may be true, but it is not the truth, and reporters and officials seldom see it the same way. . . . In the old days, the reporters or couriers of bad news were often put to the gallows; now they are given the Pulitzer Prize; but the conflict goes on.

—*James Reston*

The news on an ordinary day [is] a strange assembly that swoops down on one's life like cousins from Oslo one has never seen before, will never see again, and who, between planes, thought they would call to say hello.

—*Roger Rosenblatt*

Wherever there are few resident correspondents, a Parkinson's Law of Journalism holds that news increases in direct proportion to the number of visiting reporters in town.

—*Mort Rosenblum*

The news has become a matter of opinion.

—Salman Rushdie

The nature of bad news infects the teller.

—William Shakespeare, Cleopatra

Though it be honest, it is never good to bring bad news.

—William Shakespeare, Cleopatra

The first bringer of unwelcome news
Hath but a losing office.

—William Shakespeare, Henry IV, Part 2

We might as well face it. The line between the news business and show business has been erased forever.

—Charles Seib

One big trouble with news is that nobody knows what it is. The other trouble is that nobody knows what it means.

—Leon Sigal

Telegraph fully all news you can get, and when there is no news send rumors.

—Wilbur F. Storey (attributed), Chicago Times *editor;*
supposedly an instruction he gave a reporter

If a tree falls in the forest and it isn't on the six o'clock news, did it actually fall?

—Kevin Sweeney

In times of calamity any rumor is believed.

—Publilius Syrus

To a philosopher all news, as it is called, is gossip, and they who edit and read it are old women over their tea.

—Henry David Thoreau

News: Things that people don't want to be known.

—*Nicolas Tomalin*

If some great catastrophe is not announced every morning, we feel a certain void. "Nothing in the paper today," we sigh.

—*Paul Valéry*

What is different now [compared with] 1960 is you have a 24-hour-a-day news cycle, a huge electronic tapeworm that has to be fed all the time.

—*Sander Vanocur*

When we hear news we should always wait for the sacrament of confirmation.

—*Voltaire*

News is what a chap who doesn't care much about anything wants to read. And it's only news until he's read it. After that it's dead.

—*Evelyn Waugh*

Like it or not, we must have the news. For if the people do not have the face of the age set clearly before them they begin to imagine it.

—*Rebecca West*

See also *Television News*

Newspapers

I keep reading between the lies.

—Goodman Ace

He had been kicked in the head by a mule when he was young, and believed everything he read in the Sunday papers.

—George Ade

I never read the papers. I haven't read a paper since I married. I rely on Sven to tell me if there's a war broken out. No, I think there's far too much going on already without reading about it as well.

—Alan Ayckbourn, Joking Apart

He who is without a newspaper is cut off from his species.

—P. T. Barnum

At certain times each year, we journalists do almost nothing except apply for the Pulitzers and several dozen other major prizes. During these times you could walk right into most newsrooms and commit a multiple axe murder naked, and it wouldn't get reported in the paper because the reporters and editors would all be too busy filling out prize applications.

—Dave Barry

The days when we could do newspapering our way, and tell the world to go to hell if it didn't like the results, are gone forever.

—James K. Batten

I am unable to understand how a man of honor could take a newspaper in his hands without a shudder of disgust.

—*Charles Baudelaire*

Newspapers are the schoolmasters of the common people. That endless book, the newspaper, is our national glory.

—*Henry Ward Beecher*

A newspaper can send more souls to heaven, and save more from hell, than all the churches or chapels in New York—besides making money at the same time. Let it be tried.

—*James Gordon Bennett Sr.*

I read the newspaper avidly. It is my one form of continuous fiction.

—*Aneurin Bevan*

The newspaper business is the only enterprise in the world where a man is expected to become an expert on any conceivable subject between 1 o'clock in the afternoon and a 6 P.M. deadline.

—*Robert S. Bird*

There is not one shred of evidence that the Internet has had any downward influence on North American or European newspaper circulation.

—*Conrad Black*

In its expanding feature content, the daily press increasingly partakes of the character of the magazine—non-threatening and easy to take. Embedded in a tissue of gourmet recipes, instruction on furniture repair, and counsel on premarital sex, the breaking (and unsettling) news is swathed in reassurances.

—*Leo Bogart*

The newspaper is one of the foremost wonders of the modern world. The family that does not take, and carefully read, at least one newspaper, is not living in the nineteenth century.

—J. A. Broadus, 1827-1895

Histories are a kind of distilled newspapers.

—Thomas Carlyle

Next to its reputation for accuracy and fairness, a publication's greatest asset is its personality. Every publication has a personality—the complex of a thousand qualities that make that publication seem like an old friend to its regular readers. You show me a successful publication and I'll show you one with a clear, distinct, consistent personality. . . . Show me a newspaper in trouble and I'll show you one with an indistinct personality, or a personality that's become outmoded or has been changed rapidly.

—William G. Connolly

With newspapers, there is sometimes disorder; without them, there is always slavery.

—Benjamin Constant

There's nothing much wrong with American newspapers today except us publishers.

—John Cowles, 1938

Viewing with dismay the conditions in somebody else's backyard is the speciality of *The New York Times*.

—John Crosby

The job of the newspaper is to comfort the afflicted and afflict the comfortable.

—Finley Peter Dunne ("Mr. Dooley")

Newspaper: Consists of just the same number of words, whether there be any news in it or not.

—*Henry Fielding*

The occupational disease among newspaper proprietors is megalomania.

—*Michael Foot*

My brother had in 1720 or '21, begun to print a newspaper. It was the second that appear'd in America and was called *The New England Courant.* I remember his being dissuaded by some of his friends from the undertaking as not likely to succeed, one newspaper being in their judgment enough for America.

—*Benjamin Franklin*

Never argue with a man who buys ink by the barrel.

—*Bill Greener*

Do not put stock in newspapers; you can find out more just by lookin' around at what is going on.

—*Forrest Gump*

Trying to determine what is going on in the world by reading the newspaper is like trying to tell the time by watching the second hand of a clock.

—*Ben Hecht*

The newspaper is a moral force second only to the church. It is a political power superior to parties. It is an instrument of justice coequal with the court.

—*William Randolph Hearst*

When I started out, people were afraid of parish priests. Now they're afraid of newspaper editors.

—*Michael D. Higgins, Irish politician (attributed)*

In newspaper work you have to learn to forget every day what happened the day before. . . . Newspaper work is valuable up until the point that is forcibly begins to destroy your memory. A writer must leave it before that point. But he will always have the scars from it. Just as any experience of war is invaluable to a writer. But it is destructive if he has too much . . .

—Ernest Hemingway

Newspapers are a bad habit, the reading equivalent of junk food.

—John Irving, A Prayer for Owen Meany

I deplore the putrid state into which the newspapers have passed and the malignity, the vulgarity and the mendacious spirit of those who write them.

—Thomas Jefferson

I do not take a single newspaper, nor read one a month, and I feel myself infinitely the happier for it.

—Thomas Jefferson

The man who never looks into a newspaper is better informed than he who reads them, inasmuch as he who knows nothing is nearer to truth than he whose mind is filled with falsehood and errors.

—Thomas Jefferson

With the possible exception of the comics, everything a newspaper used to do somebody else is doing more quickly, more attractively, more efficiently, and in a more interesting and unfettered way.

—Jon Katz

You are full of enthusiasm for the eternal verities—life is worth living, and then out of sinful curiosity you open a newspaper. You are disillusioned and wrecked.

—Patrick Kavanagh

No new medium has ever replaced an existing medium in the history of mass communications. Those who say newspapers are dinosaurs are wrong; newspapers still have a very important role to play in a democratic society.

—William B. Ketter

The smell of death permeates the newspaper business these days.

—Howard Kurtz, 1993

The window to the world can be covered by a newspaper.

—Stanislaw Lec

A device for amusing one half of the world with the other half's troubles.

—Leonard Louis Levinson

You should always believe all you read in the newspaper, as this makes them more interesting.

—Rose Macaulay

The newspaper is an institution developed by modern civilization to present the news of the day, to foster commerce and industry through widely circulated advertisements and to furnish that check upon government which no constitution has ever been able to provide.

—Robert McCormick

All successful newspapers are ceaselessly querulous and bellicose. They never defend anyone or anything if they can help it; if the job is forced upon them, they tackle it by denouncing someone or something else.

—H. L. Mencken

Whenever I see a newspaper, I think of the poor trees. As trees they provide beauty, shade and shelter, but as paper all they provide is rubbish.

—Yehudi Menuhin

A good newspaper is a nation talking to itself.

—*Arthur Miller*

I read the newspapers to see how God governs the world.

—*John Newton*

One of the chief enemies of the Kingdom of God.

—*Northwest Conference of the
Methodist Episcopal church*

If a newspaper prints a sex crime, it's smut, but when *The New York Times* prints it, it's a sociological study.

—*Adolph S. Ochs*

A newspaper should have no friends.

—*Joseph Pulitzer*

The front page is a paper's most precious commodity. It helps set the nation's agenda.

—*Jonathan Power*

All I know is what I read in the papers.

—*Will Rogers*

The careful reader of a few good newspapers can learn more in a year than most scholars in their libraries.

—*F. B. Sanborn*

The newspaper is the second hand in the clock of history; and it is not only made of baser metal than those which point to the minute and the hour, but it seldom goes right.

—*Arthur Schopenhauer*

Ever notice that no matter what happens in one day, it exactly fits in the newspaper?

—*Jerry Seinfeld*

148

Newspapers are unable, seemingly, to discriminate between a bicycle accident and the collapse of a civilization.

—George Bernard Shaw

The newspapers! Sir, they are the most villainous—licentious abominable—infernal—not that I ever read them—no—I make it a rule never to look into a newspaper.

—Richard Brinsley Sheridan

Newspapers should be the modern-day church doors on which any and all can post their theses.

—Dick Smyser

It is better to appear in hell than in the newspapers.

—Spanish proverb

The newspaper is a microcosm of the national life. This is as much the case in regard to the advertisements as to the letter-press. A glance over the advertising columns of a large . . . paper shows reflected, as it were in a mirror, the whole of the active life of the people.

—W. Stead Jr.

I'm with you on the free press. It's the newspapers I can't stand.

—Tom Stoppard, Night and Day

It is a newspaper's duty to print the news and raise hell.

—Wilbur F. Storey, 1861

It is part of the social mission of every great newspaper to provide a refuge and a home for the largest possible number of salaried eccentrics.

—Lord Thomson

And I am sure that I never read any memorable news in a newspaper. If we read of one man robbed, or murdered, or killed by accident . . . we never need read another. One is enough. If you are acquainted with the principle, what do you care for a myriad instances and applications.

—Henry David Thoreau

Blessed be they who never see a newspaper, for they shall see Nature, and, through her, God.

—Henry David Thoreau

Newspapers would be better if they had no publishers, no advertisers and no readers. Then journalists could make a hell of a paper.

—Sérgio Vaz

It is a serious, sacred business. . . . A newspaper, like Caesar's wife, must be above suspicion.

—Joseph Ward

There are three things that no one else can do to the entire satisfaction of anyone else: make love, poke the fire, and run a newspaper.

—William Allen White

Newspapers are unique barometers of their age. They indicate more plainly than anything else the climate of the societies to which they belong.

—Francis Williams

A newspaper, like a theatre, must mainly owe its continuance in life to the fact that it pleases many persons; and in order to please many persons it will, unconsciously perhaps, respond to their several tastes, reflect their various qualities, and reproduce their views. In a certain sense it is evolved out of the community that absorbs it, and, therefore, partaking of the character of the community, while it may retain many merits and virtues, it will display itself, as in some respects ignorant, trivial, narrow, and vulgar.

—*William Winter, 1889*

See also *Journalism, Journalists; News; Readers*

Photojournalism and Photographers

Photography helps people to see.

—Berenice Abbott

If [a photograph] does something to you . . . if it makes you laugh, if it makes you cry, if it rips out your heart, then it's a good picture.

—Eddie Adams, Pulitzer Prize-winning photographer

You are a pest, by the very nature of that camera in your hand.

—Princess Anne

If you saw a man drowning and you could either save him or photograph the event, what kind of film would you use?

—Anonymous

There are things nobody would see if I didn't photograph them.

—Diane Arbus

The camera is the eye of history. . . . You must never make bad pictures.

—Mathew Brady, pioneering Civil War photographer

For me, there is only one criterion for a good photograph: that it be unforgettable.

—Brassaï

I visualize the day when we will be sending pictures over our own leased wire system, just as we now send the news.

—*Kent Cooper, AP general manager, 1926*

The paparazzi are nothing but dogs of war.

—*Catherine Deneuve, following Princess Diana's death*

I know it's just a job they have to do, but sometimes I wish they wouldn't.

—*Princess Diana*

The art of news photography is much more than the pressing of a cable release, the adjusting of scales and shutters and the sighting of an object through a viewfinder. It is the ability of the news cameraman to go beyond the mechanics of exact procedure, and feel, sense and record the story with the vividness of the news gatherer.

—*A. J. Erickson*

The camera cannot lie. But it can be an accessory to untruth.

—*Harold Evans*

In this age of the great electronic blur, it is imperative that we seek solace in the eloquent silence and permanence of the still photograph. A still photograph forces us to be still. It compels us to consider an observed moment and, in turn, to feel it, to react, to reflect—or to take action. In its own stubborn, point-blank manner, great photojournalism conveys something resembling tangible truth. Unlike any other medium, it says concisely and directly: Stop, damn it, and witness what I have witnessed.

—*David Friend*

Photography is the only "language" understood in all parts of the world, and bridging all nations and cultures, it links the family of man. Independent of political influence—where people are free—it reflects truthfully life and events, allows us to share in the hopes and despair of others and illuminates political and social conditions. We become the eye-witnesses of the humanity and inhumanity of mankind . . .

—*Helmut Gernsheim*

I'm not sure that what people want any more is photojournalism. It's becoming an art form that has very little impact on the public, rather than a useful communications tool. You don't hear about people holding a picture up in Congress and demanding that something be done. People are just not affected.

—*Mark Godfrey*

Photography is a tool for dealing with things everybody knows about but isn't attending to.

—*Emmit Gowin*

If I could tell the story in words, I wouldn't need to lug a camera.

—*Lewis Hine*

Once you can manipulate pictures on a computer you can't believe them any more. There will be no more Cartier-Bressons.

—*David Hockney*

The camera is an instrument that teaches people how to see without a camera.

—*Dorothea Lange*

"There are no paparazzi here."

—*Jennifer Lopez, on what she'd like*
God to say when she arrives in heaven

Photographers are the most loathsome inconvenience. They're merciless. They're the pits.

—*Paul Newman*

The Spanish War first showed what could be achieved by daring and resourceful photographers who were ready to touch elbows with soldiers and sailors in action. The public at home welcomed this new manner of illustration, and the newspapers and magazines made it profitable for the men who could "deliver the goods," to make war-photography a profession.

—Outing *magazine, September 1905*

One of our jobs as photojournalists is to bear witness.

—*Steve Raymer*

I like photographers—you don't ask questions.

—*Ronald Reagan*

I recall a midnight expedition to the Mulberry Bend with the sanitary police that had turned up a couple of characteristic cases of overcrowding. . . . When the report was submitted to the Health Board the next day, it did not make much of an impression—these things rarely do, put in mere words—until my negatives, still dripping from the darkroom, came to reinforce them. From them there was no appeal.

—*Jacob Riis*

As long as there's journalism, there will be photojournalism. They're two halves of a whole. And although they certainly won't last forever, for the moment I don't see either one of them coming to an end.

—*Sebastião Salgado*

Instead of just recording reality, photographs have become the norm for the way things appear to us, thereby changing the very idea of reality and of realism.

—*Susan Sontag*

Photography records the gamut of feelings written on the human face; the beauty of the earth and skies that man has inherited; and the wealth and confusion man has created. It is a major force in explaining man to man.

—Edward Steichen

Photography is now a "fad," and the "fadders" are not alone those who earn their livings by making faces, etcetera. Again, instead of the representatives of the press feeling loath to speak a word of praise for photography, or even to credit it with any of its good works and achievements, the youthful reporter of today . . . cannot secure a position unless he can swing a photographic vocabulary and press a button.

—Wilson's Photographic Magazine, *April 1893*

I photograph to find out what something will look like photographed.

—Garry Winogrand

Photography is the science of writing with light.

—George Yates

See also *TV; TV News*

Politics, Politicians and the Media

Politicians have a higher claim to speak for the people than journalists.

—John Birt

Numerous politicians have seized absolute power and muzzled the press. Never in history has the press seized absolute power and muzzled the politicians.

—David Brinkley

Since I write a humor column I have a vested interest in a free press. I don't seem to have any problem making fun of the President of the United States, the Cabinet, Congress, the CIA and the FBI. I don't know if our leaders read the column or not, but since I've been writing it I have had no visits from anyone in a raincoat telling me I better knock it off. The people who attempt to do the same thing I am doing in 95 percent of the world are either in gulags under house arrest or are jobless. For some reason not too many governments can handle satire. My heroes in the world are the men and women in these countries who, knowing the consequences, persist in holding up their leaders to ridicule.

—Art Buchwald

Politics and the media are inseparable. It is only the politicians and the media that are incompatible.

—Walter Cronkite

1952 was the last year that television covered a political event as if television weren't there.

> —*Walter Cronkite*

My first bit of advice [to new senators] would be: Get a great press secretary.

> —*Alfonse D'Amato*

Keep the press off the plane.

> —*Robert Dole, withdrawing from the*
> *1988 presidential race, when saying how he*
> *would have run his campaign differently*

The hardest people to interview are politicians. They don't have the words "yes" and "no" in their vocabularies. They qualify everything.

> —*Mike Douglas*

Nearly all of our political comment originates in Washington. Washington politicians, after talking things over with each other, relay misinformation to Washington journalists who, after further intramural discussion, print it where it is thoughtfully read by the same politicians. It is the only completely successful system for the recycling of garbage that has yet been devised.

> —*John Kenneth Galbraith*

Practice whatever the big truth is so that you can say it in forty seconds on camera.

> —*Newt Gingrich*

I never ask for fairness in the media, only mercy.

> —*Phil Gramm*

The only way with newspaper attacks is, as the Irish say, "to keep never minding." This has been my practice through life.

> —*Charles Gray, British Prime Minister, 1834*

We're all going to have to seriously question the system for selecting our national leaders, for it reduces the press of this nation to hunters and presidential candidates to being hunted.

—*Gary Hart*

Relations between politicians and the press have deteriorated, are deteriorating, and should on no account be allowed to improve.

—*Sidney Jacobson, English editor*

Television has shortened our political discourse.

—*Kathleen Hall Jamieson*

My great wish is to go on in a strict but silent performance of my duty; to avoid attracting notice and to keep my name out of the newpapers.

—*Thomas Jefferson, 1789*

Through the constant media focus on today—not yesterday, not tomorrow—every issue was magnified and simplified. Politicians were under constant media pressure to respond immediately on short-term problems. And woe to them if they didn't; failure to react brought a chorus of media criticism.

—*Haynes Johnson*

There is but one way for a newspaperman to look at a politician and that is down.

—*Frank Kent (attributed to others)*

We are going to have to endure an imperial media with a government by public opinion poll.

—*Michael Ledeen*

They're just a bunch of goddamn animals. Why the hell should I have to put up with all their shenanigans, anyway? I'm the mayor and if I want them out of my office, out they go.

—*John Lindsay*

If you don't have regular care and feeding of the press, they will eat you.

—Trent Lott

The press is to be used as a mirror in which public figures can see whether they are on the right track.

—Nelson Mandela

Speaking from my own experience, I believe that it is when leading media figures see too much rather than too little of prime ministers that the freedom of the press is endangered.

—James Margach, British journalist

With the coming of television, and the knowledge of how it could be used to seduce voters, the old political values disappeared. Something new, murky and undefined started to rise from the mists. . . . Style becomes substance. The medium is the massage and the masseur gets the votes.

—Joe McGinniss

In the television age, the key distinction is between the candidate who can speak poetry and the one who can only speak prose.

—Richard M. Nixon

You know very well that whether you are on page one or page thirty depends on whether they fear you. It is just as simple as that.

—Richard M. Nixon

You won't have Nixon to kick around anymore, because, gentlemen, this is my last press conference.

—Richard M. Nixon, to reporters after
losing the California governor's race in 1962.

Never lose your temper with the press or the public is a major rule of political life.

—*Christabel Pankhurst*

Much like the gingham dog and the calico cat of poetic fame, the press and politicians eat each other up until public trust for both disappears.

—*Elaine Povich*

Politicians who complain about the media are like ships' captains who complain about the sea.

—*Enoch Powell*

Politicians waste little love on the newspeople who cover them, and the newspeople display a surly skepticism towards politicians as a badge of honor. Yet if the voters I met on the campaign trail are any indication (and poll data suggest that they are), much of the public has lumped newspeople and politicians together into a single class, which, increasingly, it despises. Respect for the government and respect for the news media have declined in tandem.

—*Jonathan Schell*

We are getting to the point where a politician will be able to run against the news media as he used to run against Communism, crime or corruption—issues no longer available to some of them.

—*Daniel Schorr*

My constituents don't know how to read, but they can't help seeing them damned pictures.
—*William Marcy Tweed, corrupt 19th century New York*
politician, on Thomas Nast's cartoon campaign against
him

See also See also *Democracy and the Media; Government and the Media; Presidents, the Presidency and the Media*

Power and Influence

The American mass media have achieved what American political might could not: the attainment for America of world domination.

—*Akbar S. Ahmed*

What the proprietorship of these newspapers is aiming at is power, and power without responsibility, the privilege of the harlot throughout the ages.

—*Stanley Baldwin*

That's the press [you hear over the phone], baby. The press. And there's nothing you can do about it.

—*Humphrey Bogart, in "Deadline USA"*

The press is a sort of wild animal in our midst—restless, gigantic, always seeking new ways to use its strength.

—*Zechariah Chafee*

CNN is one of the participants in the [Gulf] war. I have a fantasy where Ted Turner is elected president but refuses because he doesn't want to give up power.

—*Arthur C. Clarke*

[The press] may not be successful much of the time in telling people what to think, but it is stunningly successful in telling its readers what to think *about*.

—*Bernard Cohen*

If newspapers are useful in overthrowing tyrants, it is only to establish a tyranny of their own.

—James Fenimore Cooper

I care not who makes the laws or the money iv a counthry so long as I run th' presses.

—Finley Peter Dunne

Madame, we are the press. You know our power; we fix all values. We set all standards. Your entire future depends on us.

—Jean Giradoux, The Madwoman of Chaillot

If this country ever fails—if this country ever becomes history—some future historian will blame it mostly on the media.

—Barry Goldwater

The hand that rules the press, the radio, the screen, and the far-spread magazine rules the country; whether we like it or not, we must learn to accept it.

—Learned Hand

Someone—was it Burke?—called journalism the *fourth* estate. In his time, that was doubtless true. But in our time, it is actually the *only* estate. It has gobbled up the other three. The lay nobility says nothing, the bishops have nothing to say, and the House of Commons has nothing to say, and says it. Journalism rules us.

—Karl Kraus

The mass media confer status. . . . Enhanced status accrues to those who merely receive attention in the media, quite apart from any editorial support. The mass media bestow prestige and enhance the authority of individuals and groups by legitimizing their status. Recognition by the press . . . testifies that one has arrived.

—Paul Lazarsfeld and Robert Merton

The power to determine each day what shall be important and what shall be neglected is power unlike any that has been exercised since the Pope lost his hold on the secular mind.

—Walter Lippmann

The media [are] the most powerful entity on earth. . . . They have the power to make the innocent guilty and to make the guilty innocent . . . because they control the minds of the masses.

—Malcolm X

We are the most powerful men in the history of the world, and I'm happy to say that, on the whole, I think that power is being used in the best interests of everybody.

—Minnesota TV news executive

I guess television just has more power than any of us know.

—Ronald Reagan

What must astonish people with casual beliefs in the vast power of the media is how difficult it is to measure media influence.

—Michael Schudson, media scholar

See also *Democracy and the Media; Government and the Media; Miscellaneous; Presidents, the Presidency and the Media*

Presidents, the Presidency and the Media

Avoid this crowd the media like the plague. And if they quote you, make damn sure they heard you.

—Barbara Bush, advice to Hilary Clinton, 1992

The White House press corps, in the main, are a bunch of prima donnas. I thought that kids in high schools asked better questions.

—Jimmy Carter

I hardly have any time to read the news anymore. Mostly, I just skim the retractions.

—Bill Clinton

I have . . . not gotten one damn bit of credit from the knee-jerk liberal press. I am damn sick and tired of it.

—Bill Clinton

Well, when you come down to it, I don't see what a reporter could do to a president, do you?

—Dwight Eisenhower

A revered president, long since dead, once told me that there . . . never would be a president who could satisfy the press until he was twenty years dead.

—Herbert Hoover

The President of the United States will not stand and be questioned like a chicken thief by men whose names he does not even know.

—Herbert Hoover

If one morning I walked on top of the water across the Potomac River, the headline that afternoon would read: "President Can't Swim."

—Lyndon B. Johnson

Whenever I was upset by something in the papers, [Jack] always told me to be more tolerant, like a horse flicking away flies in the summer.

—Jacqueline Kennedy

Maybe if you had printed more about the [Bay of Pigs] operation, you would have saved us from a colossal mistake.

—John F. Kennedy

We wouldn't have had a prayer without that gadget.

—John F. Kennedy, on TV's role
in his presidential campaign

Cronyism is the curse of journalism. After many years I have reached the firm conclusion that it is impossible for any objective newspaperman to be a friend of a president.

—Walter Lippmann

Abraham Lincoln would not have been able to prosecute the Civil War to a successful conclusion had television been flooding the contemporary scene with daily pictures of the northern Copperheads who opposed the war, of the draft riots that rocketed through northern cities, and especially of the stark horror of Vicksburg. Sometime late in 1862 he would have been forced to capitulate, with the probability that slavery would have continued in the southern states till the early years of [the 20th] century.

—James Michener

[A President] may make a formal address, hold a press conference, consent to an interview, telephone an astronaut, go to a football game, receive a visiting head of state, take a trip abroad, or play with his dog on the White House lawn. He may send his family, his cabinet members, or his political allies before the cameras. In almost every case, he, and he alone, decides. His ability to choose when and how to appear without cost before millions of viewers is completely unmatched by his political or Congressional opponents.

—Newton Minow

If we treat the press with a little more contempt we'll probably get better treatment.

—Richard M. Nixon

The media are far more powerful than the President in creating public awareness and shaping public opinion, for the simple reason that the media always have the last word.

—Richard M. Nixon

People in the media say they must look . . . at the President with a microscope. Now, I don't mind a microscope, but boy, when they use a proctoscope, that's going too far.

—Richard M. Nixon

By August 1979, if the President [Jimmy Carter] had been set upon by a pack of wild dogs, a good portion of the press would have sided with the dogs and declared that he provoked the attack.

—Jody Powell

I was going to have an opening statement but I decided I wanted a lot of attention so I decided to wait and "leak" it.

—Ronald Reagan

I'd like to go back to those days when the press never quoted the President without permission.

—Ronald Reagan

There are really only three ways [for Presidents] to deal with the press. The best way is to tell them everything: this keeps them busy and eventually exhausts and bores them. The next best way is to tell them nothing, which at least excites the cop in them and gives them the excitement of a mystery. The worst way, which is Mr Nixon's way and also Mr Johnson's way, is to try to manipulate them, to pretend to be candid in private conversation, but to use every trick in the book to get them to fill the headlines and front pages with calculated trash.

—James Reston

The relationship between a reporter and a President is exactly the same as that between a pitcher and a batter. . . . They both are trying to keep each other away.

—Merriman Smith

You don't tell us how to stage the news, and we don't tell you how to cover it.

—Larry Speakes, press secretary for
Ronald Reagan; sign on his desk

The people elected me—not the press.

—William H. Taft

I always learned more about what was on the minds of the people from the reporters' questions than they could possibly learn from me.

—Harry S. Truman

To hell with them. When history is written, they will be the sons of bitches—not I.

—Harry S Truman, on the press

As the age of television progresses the Reagans will be the rule, not the exception. To be perfect for television is all a President has to be these days.

—Gore Vidal (attributed)

From the beginning of his presidency, Mr. Reagan and his aides have understood and exploited what they acknowledge to be the built-in tendency of television to emphasize appearances and impressions more than information. Central to the President's overall strategy has been his unusual ability to deal with television and print reporters on his terms—to decide when, where, and how he will engage them. In short, the art of controlled access.

—Steven R. Weisman

In America the president reigns for four years, and journalism governs for ever and ever.

—Oscar Wilde

See also *Democracy and the Media; Government and the Media; Politics, Politicians and the Media; Power and Influence*

The Press

But none of the means of communication are more sacred, or have been cherished with more tenderness and care by settlers of America, than the press.

—John Quincy Adams

The press is the living jury of the nation.

—James Gordon Bennett Sr.

The failures of the press have contributed immensely to the emergence of a talk-show nation, in which public discourse is reduced to ranting and raving and posturing.

—Carl Bernstein

The press has become the modern equivalent of peer group pressure.

—Rose Bird

The sovereign press for the most part acknowledges accountability to no one except its owners and publishers.

—Zechariah Chafee Jr.

I am always in favor of the free press but sometimes they say quite nasty things.

—Winston Churchill

The press, like fire, is an excellent servant, but a terrible master.

—James Fenimore Cooper

Thou god of our idolatry, the press.

—*William Cowper*

People who don't understand the press fear it. People who do understand it fear it even more.

—*Jack DeVore*

The press doesn't exist in America to be liked. But . . . more and more people consider the media to be a part of what's destroying our country.

—*Susan Estrich*

The role of the press is to inform society about problems, not to solve them.

—*Reuven Frank*

One of the things the press is not covering well is the general boredom of the public.

—*Henry Graff*

The press in its historic connotation comprehends every sort of publication which affords a vehicle of information and opinion.

—*Charles Evans Hughes*

The newspapers of this country by their abandoned spirit of falsehood have more effectually destroyed the utility of the press than all the shackles devised by Bonaparte.

—*Thomas Jefferson*

The press is our chief ideological weapon.

—*Nikita S. Khrushchev*

In the beginning was the press, and then the world appeared.

—*Karl Kraus*

The press is like the peculiar uncle you keep in the attic—just one of those unfortunate things.

—G. Gordon Liddy

The American press makes me think of a gigantic, super-modern fish cannery, a hundred floors high, capitalized at eleven billion dollars, and with tens of thousands of workers standing ready at the canning machines, but relying for its raw material on an inadequate number of handline fishermen in leaky rowboats.

—A. J. Liebling

The gallery in which the reporters sit has become a fourth estate of the realm.

—Thomas Macaulay

To the press alone, checkered as it is with abuses, the world is indebted for all the triumphs which have been obtained by reason and humanity over error and oppression.

—James Madison

No nation is so poor that it cannot afford a free press. In fact, the poorer you are, the more you need a free press.

—Surin Pitsuwan, Thailand Minister of Foreign Affairs

The press: A chartered libertine.

—William Pitt

Of all the institutions in our inordinately complacent society, none is so addicted as the press to self-righteousness, self-satisfaction and self-congratulation.

—Abe Raskin

The press in this country is now, and always has been, so thoroughly dominated by the wealthy few of the country that it cannot be depended upon to give the great mass of the people that correct information concerning political, economical and social subjects which it is necessary that the mass of people shall have in order that they shall vote and in all ways act in the best way to protect themselves from the brutal force and chicanery of the ruling and employing classes . . .

—E. W. Scripps

Hastiness and superficiality are the psychic diseases of the twentieth century, and more than anywhere else this disease is reflected in the press.

—Alexander Solzhenitsyn

The press is an enormous machinery for misdirecting creative energy.

—Stephen Spender

The worst fault of the press today is not partisanship but trivialization. The one-newspaper city is often starved for world news or issues analysis. A lot of readers are being malnourished on a thought-free diet.

—Richard Strout

See also *Newspapers*

Print and Printing

It is well to observe the force and virtue and consequence of discoveries, and these are to be seen nowhere more conspicuously than in those three which were unknown to the ancients, and of which the origin, though recent, is obscure and inglorious; namely, printing, gunpowder and magnet [i.e. the Mariner's Needle]. From these three have changed the whole face and state of things throughout the world.

—Francis Bacon

The printing press is either the greatest blessing or the greatest curse of modern times, one sometimes forgets which.

—James Barrie

I thank God we have no free schools or printing; and I hope that we shall not have them these hundred years. For learning has brought disobedience and heresy and sects into the world; and printing has divulged them and libels against the government. God keep us from them both.

—William Berkeley, Governor of Virginia, 1671

Printing: A multiplication of mind.

—Richard Carlile

The three greatest inventions of modern civilization, gunpowder, printing, and the Protestant religion.

—Thomas Carlyle

Printing broke out in the province of Kansu in 868 A.D. The early Chinese simply could not let well enough alone.

—*Will Cuppy*

Reading off the screen is still vastly inferior to reading off of paper. Even I, who have these expensive screens and fancy myself as a pioneer of this Web lifestyle, when it comes to something over about four or five pages, I print it out and carry it around with me and annotate. And it's quite a hurdle for technology to achieve to match that level of usability.

—*Bill Gates*

Publishers are a band of panderers which sprang into existence soon after the death of Gutenberg and which now overruns the world.

—*Elbert Hubbard*

What gunpowder did for war, the printing press has done for the mind; the statesman is no longer clad in the steel of special education, but every reading man is his judge.

—*Wendell Phillips*

Providence . . . permitted the invention of printing as a scourge for the sins of the people.

—*Alexander Pope*

Print is the sharpest and the strongest weapon of our party.

—*Joseph Stalin*

The most powerful weapon of ignorance—the diffusion of printed material.

—*Leo Tolstoy*

The invention of printing added a new element of power to the race. From that hour the brain and not the arm, the thinker and not the soldier, books and not kings, were to rule the world;

and weapons, forged in the mind, keen-edged and brighter than the sunbeam, were to supplant the sword and the battle-ax.

—E. P. Whipple

This new invention of printing has produced various effects of which your Holiness cannot be ignorant. If it has restored books and learning, it has also been the occasion of those sects and schisms which appear daily.

—Cardinal Wolsey, writing to Pope Clement VII

Propaganda

What is truth? We must adopt a pragmatic definition: it is what is believed to be the truth. A lie that is put across therefore becomes the truth and may, therefore, be justified. The difficulty is to keep up lying . . . it is simpler to tell the truth and if a sufficient emergency arises, to tell one, big thumping lie that will then be believed.

—British Ministry of Information

Propaganda is the art of persuading others of what one does not believe oneself.

—Abba Eban

Once we have cast another group in the role of the enemy, we know that they are to be distrusted—that they are evil incarnate. We then twist all their communication to fit our belief.

—Jerome D. Frank

It is the absolute right of the state to supervise the formation of public opinion.

—Joseph Goebbels

Naturally the common people don't want war . . . but after all it is the leaders of a country who determine policy, and it is always a simple matter to drag the people along, whether it is a democracy, or a fascist dictatorship, or a parliament or a communist dictatorship. All you have to do is tell them they are being attacked, and denounce the pacifists for lack of patriotism and exposing the country to danger. . . . It works the same in every country.

—Hermann Göring

All propaganda has to be popular and has to accommodate itself to the comprehension of the least intelligent of those it seeks to reach.

—Adolf Hitler

I shall give a propagandist reason for starting the war, no matter whether it is plausible or not.

—Adolf Hitler

The great masses of the people will more easily fall victims to a great lie than to a small lie.

—Adolf Hitler

The victor will not be asked afterwards whether he told the truth or not. When starting and waging war it is not right that matters, but victory.

—Adolf Hitler

Through clever and constant propaganda, people can be made to see paradise as hell and vice versa, to consider the most wretched sort of life as heaven itself.

—Adolf Hitler

The greatest triumphs of propaganda have been accomplished, not by doing something, but by refraining from doing. Great is truth, but still greater, from a practical point of view, is silence about truth.

—Aldous Huxley

The propagandist's purpose is to make one set of people forget that other sets of people are human.

—Aldous Huxley

Propaganda

All our advertising is propaganda, of course, but it has become so much a part of our life, is so pervasive, that we just don't know what it is propaganda for.

—*Pauline Kael*

Since crowds do not reason, they can only be organized and stimulated through symbols and phrases.

—*Ivy Lee*

We must remember that in time of war what is said on the enemy's side of the front is always propaganda and what is said on our side of the front is truth and righteousness, the cause of humanity and a crusade for peace.

—*Walter Lippmann*

And if, to be sure, sometimes you need to conceal a fact with words, do it in such a way that it does not become known, or, if it does become known, that you have a ready and quick defense.

—*Machiavelli*

The mass of mankind is always swayed by appearances.

—*Machiavelli*

How good bad music and bad reasons sound when we march against an enemy.

—*Friedrich Nietzsche*

All propaganda is lies, even when one is telling the truth.

—*George Orwell*

He who has a message and no propaganda will not get very far.

—*Joel Augustus Rogers*

Why is propaganda so much more successful when it stirs up hatred than when it tries to stir up friendly feeling?

—*Bertrand Russell*

It's the inherent right of the government to lie to save itself.
—*Arthur D. Sylvester*

To succeed in chaining the crowd you must seem to wear the same fetters.
—*Voltaire*

See also *Advertising; Public Relations*

The Public and Public Opinion

When the people have no other tyrant, their own public opinion becomes one.

—*E. G. Bulwer-Lytton*

These are times when public opinion is the worst of all opinions.

—*Nicolas-Sebastien Chamfort*

Opinion is that exercise of the human will which helps us to make a decision without information.

—*John Erskine*

The country is somehow held together by celebrities. Celebrity actors. Celebrity talk-show people. Celebrity designers and politicians. It's this jungle of junk. Junk information. Junk misinformation. Half-baked knowledge. Received opinion. It's like a huge orchestra with everyone playing in a different key.

—*Buck Henry*

Too often we . . . enjoy the comfort of opinion without the discomfort of thought.

—*John F. Kennedy*

Public opinion in this country is everything.

—*Abraham Lincoln*

With public sentiment, nothing can fail; without it, nothing can succeed.

—Abraham Lincoln

The pressure of public opinion is like the pressure of the atmosphere; you can't see it—but, all the same, it is sixteen pounds to the square inch.

—James Russell Lowell

Public opinion is a compound of folly, weakness, prejudice, wrong feeling, right feeling, obstinacy and newspaper paragraphs.

—Robert Peel

There is no group in America that can withstand the force of an aroused public opinion.

—Franklin D. Roosevelt

One should as a rule respect public opinion insofar as it is necessary to avoid starvation and keep out of prison, but anything that goes beyond this is voluntary submission to an unnecessary tyranny.

—Bertrand Russell

We [the press] tell the public which way the cat is jumping. The public will take care of the cat.

—Arthur Hays Sulzburger

It requires ages to destroy a popular opinion.

—Voltaire

Public Relations

Any publicity is good publicity.

—Anonymous

I don't care what you say about me, as long as you say something about me, and as long as you say it right.

—Anonymous

Liking people is a great asset if you're a cocker spaniel, but it won't get you a job in P.R.

—Anonymous

A flack is a person who makes all or part of his income by obtaining space in newspapers without cost to himself or his clients. Usually a professional. The term also includes those persons who seek free space for causes which they deem beneficial to the country, to the nation, or to God. Mostly amateurs. Of the two categories, the pros are easier to handle. They are known formally as public relations men. . . . You do not owe the PR man anything. The owner of the newspaper, not the flack, pays your salary. Your immediate job is to serve the reader, not the man who would raid your columns.

—Associated Press Managing Editors guidelines

Live by publicity, you'll probably die by publicity.

—Russell Baker

There's no such thing as bad publicity except your own obituary.

—*Brendan Behan*

People need sacred dances. Public relations counsels should be trained to call the tune.

—*Edward L. Bernays*

Public relations is the attempt, by information, persuasion and adjustment, to engineer public support for an activity, cause, movement or institution.

—*Edward L. Bernays*

When I started, everyone was using hunch and insight, but that didn't go far enough. You have to use feedback. Today, you don't take a chance with public opinion when modern polling techniques can tell you within three percentage points why you're wearing that particular tie or color shirt.

—*Edward L. Bernays*

Public Relations: Hiring someone who knows what he is doing to convince the public that you know what you are doing.

—*Hyman Maxwell Berston*

Formerly, a public man needed a *private* secretary for a barrier between himself and the public. Nowadays he has a *press* secretary to keep him properly in the public eye.

—*Daniel J. Boorstin*

Two centuries ago when a great man appeared, people looked for God's purpose in him; today we look for his press agent.

—*Daniel J. Boorstin*

Publicity is justly commended as a remedy for social and industrial diseases. Sunlight is said to be the best of disinfectants; electric light the most efficient policeman.

—*Louis Brandeis*

To be effective and credible, public relations messages must be based on facts. Nevertheless, we are advocates, and we need to remember that. We are advocates of a particular point of view—our client's or our employer's point of view. And while we recognize that serving the public interest best serves our client's interest, we are not journalists. That's not our job.

—*Harold Burson*

Most press officers at the Pentagon wouldn't tell you if your coat was on fire.

—*Don Campbell*

A dozen press agents working overtime can do terrible things to the human spirit.

—*Cecil B. DeMille*

If you've got some news that you don't want noticed, put it out Friday afternoon at 4 P.M.

—*David Gergen*

Public relations is a preventive medicine, not a deodorant to be sprayed around where it stinks.

—*Kenneth Haagensen*

The art of publicity is a black art.

—*Learned Hand*

Public relations specialists make flower arrangements of the facts, placing them so that the wilted and less attractive petals are hidden by sturdy blooms.

—*Alan Harrington*

I don't care what is written about me so long as it isn't true.
—*Katharine Hepburn*

The development of the publicity man is a clear sign that the facts of modern life do not spontaneously take a shape in which they can be known. They must be given a shape by somebody . . .

—Walter Lippmann

Conduct public relations as if the whole company depends on it.

—Arthur W. Page

Public relations is not a peculiarly American phenomenon, but it has nowhere flourished as in the United States. Nowhere else is it so widely practiced, so lucrative, so pretentious, so respectable and disreputable, so widely suspected and so extravagantly extolled.

—J. A. R. Pimlott, British academic, 1951

Public relations helps an organization and its publics adapt mutually to each other. Public relations is an organization's efforts to win the cooperation of groups of people.

—Public Relations Society of America

Planned public relations is usually a stepchild of conflict.

—Kinsey M. Robinson

Sometimes I describe myself as a lobbyist who tries to raise certain issues and arguments before the public, the government and the press. But I am also a publisher—of books, pamphlets, reports, and issue-oriented advertisements. In addition, I am a patron of the arts and culture. I am also a corporate spokesman who explains and defends Mobil's point of view. From time to time, I am an advocate who confronts individuals and institutions whose positions are, in our view, wrong or misinformed. And I am a media critic who refuses to allow inaccurate or damaging stories to go unanswered.

—Herb Schmertz, former VP for Public Affairs at Mobil

I don't care what you say about me. Just be sure to spell my name wrong.

—*Barbra Streisand*

[T]he best PR ends up looking like news. You never know when a PR agency is being effective, you'll just find your views slowly shifting.

—*Susan Trento*

At any public relations luncheon, the quality of the food is inversely related to the quality of the information.

—*Earl Ubell*

What rage for fame attends both great and small!
Better be damned than mentioned not at all.

—*John Wolcot*

See also *Advertising; Propaganda*

Radio

Another advantage of radio is that it never shows old movies.

—Anonymous

The whole country was tied together by radio. We all experi-enced the same heroes and comedians and singers. They were giants.

—Woody Allen

I doubt if we will ever make any money [from radio]. Of course we have some hopes along that line, but I doubt if we will.

—Merlin H. Aylesworth, NBC President, 1927

Radio was really a do-it-yourself television. Instead of a big ugly glass picture tube, you saw the performers in your own mind. You were not restricted by the boundaries of a 21-inch tube, but instead painted your own big-as-life version of each moment with that loving creative brush we call imagination.

—Jack Benny

Too bad they invented radio when nobody had anything to say.

—G. K. Chesterton

[Radio:] The triumph of illiteracy.

—John Dos Passos

The power of radio is not that it speaks to millions, but that it speaks intimately and privately to each one of those millions.

—Hallie Flanagan

With the instrument of radio you can make public opinion. Perhaps even conquer a country.

—Joseph Goebbels

Radio is, indeed, the art of the imagination.

—Robert Hilliard

I believe that the quickest way to kill broadcasting would be to use it for direct advertising. The reader of the newspaper has an option whether he will read an ad or not, but if a speech by the President is to be used as the meat in a sandwich of two patent medicine advertisements there will be no radio left.

—Herbert Hoover, 1924, then Secretary of Commerce

[It is] inconceivable that we should allow so great a possibility for service and for news and for entertainment and education [as radio] . . . to be drowned in advertising chatter or used for commercial purposes.

—Herbert Hoover, 1922

Public radio is a ghetto of good taste.

—Garrison Keillor

Radio has no future.

—Lord Kelvin, ca. 1897

Radio news is bearable. This is due to the fact that while the news is being broadcast the disk jockey is not allowed to talk.

—Fran Lebowitz

This is London.

—Edward R. Murrow, signature line in his broadcasts from London in World War II

Radio lets people see things with their own ears.

—New York Times *editorial*

Radio sets are like continuously-firing automatic pistols shooting at silence.

—*Max Picard*

I have in mind a plan of development which would make radio a "household utility" in the same sense as the piano and phonograph. The idea is to bring music into the house by wireless. . . . The receiver can be designed in the form of a simple "Radio Music Box" . . . supplied with amplifying tubes and a loudspeaker telephone, all of which can be neatly mounted in one box.

—*David Sarnoff, 1916*

Radio is the creative theater of the mind.

—*"Wolfman Jack" Smith*

[Radio] is the most intimate and the most powerful medium in broadcasting.

—*Tom Snyder*

[Radio:] An instrument perfectly suited to a prison.

—*Leon Trotsky*

Ladies and gentlemen, I have a grave announcement to make. Incredible as it may seem, both the observations of science and the evidence of our eyes lead to the inescapable assumption that those strange beings who landed in the Jersey farmlands tonight are the vanguards of an invading army from the planet Mars.

—*Orson Welles's* War of the Worlds *broadcast, 1938*

I live in a strictly rural community, and people here speak of "The Radio" in the large sense, with an over-meaning. When they say "The Radio" they don't mean a cabinet, an electrical phenomenon, or a man in a studio, they refer to a pervading and somewhat godlike presence which has come into their lives and homes.

—*E. B. White, 1939*

See also *Broadcasting*

Readers and Reading

Reading is a basic tool in the living of a good life.

—Mortimer Adler

'Tis the good reader that makes the book.

—Ralph Waldo Emerson

Unless an individual spends at least one hour and 45 minutes a day reading newspapers, magazines and books, he is not going very far.

—George Gallup

In a multicultural, multimedia world, people pay attention to the media that pay attention to them.

—Felix F.Gutiérrez

Paper is patient, but the reader isn't.

—Joseph Joubert

Reading, like prayer, remains one of our few private acts.

—William Jovanovich

I think it well to remember that, when writing for the newspaper, we are writing for an elderly lady in Hastings who has two cats of which she is passionately proud. Unless our stuff can successfully compete for her interest with those cats, it is no good.

—Wilmott Lewis

Readers are plentiful, thinkers are rare.

—Harriet Martineau

I've never known any trouble that an hour's reading didn't assuage.

—Montesquieu

I don't give a damn what the media critics say. It's what your readers say. If you haven't got any readers, you're only talking to yourself.

—Rupert Murdoch

The reaction of journalists was amusing to me, but not really meaningful. Obviously we never designed *USA Today* for journalists. We were after readers.

—Al Neuharth

It is *hard* news that catches readers. Features hold them.

—Lord Northcliffe

We have gotten complacent. We neither funded nor demanded the quality our readers require in an era of proliferating media choices. We shouldn't be surprised, then, if we lose readers of a newspaper that you can flip through in ten minutes and leave feeling undernourished.

—Eugene Patterson

Most people buy a particular paper not so much because it represents their views as because it provides them with what they need without actively annoying them.

—Gerald Priestland

There is now a vast crowd that is a permanent audience waiting to be amused, cash customers screaming for their money's worth, all fixed in a consumer's attitude. They look on at more and more, and join in less and less.

—J. B. Priestley

Along with the responsible editors we must have responsible *readers*. No matter how conscientiously the publisher and his associates perform their work, they can do only half the job. Readers must do the rest. The fountain serves no useful purpose if the horse refuses to drink.

—Arthur Hays Sulzburger

Half of the American people never read a newspaper. Half never voted for president. One hopes it is the same half.

—Gore Vidal

I want to get the whole country reading again.

—Oprah Winfrey, on promoting books on her talk show

Think of women as a suburb you don't cover very well. . . . If your newspaper didn't cover a suburb, it wouldn't surprise you that readership is not there. So why are we surprised when women are buying less and less?

—Nancy J. Woodhull

See also *Sources*

Recording Industry

The record industry has failed to dam the digital stream, and the ways we find, buy, and experience recorded music will be changing drastically.

—Dave Battino and Kelli Richards

You can't buy a CD with songs about guns [at Wal-Mart], but you can trot over to the other side of the store and buy a gun.

—Jello Biafra

Here I was . . . at a major record company [listed] on the New York Stock Exchange signing . . . artists whose appeal was almost inherently based on eschewing materialism.

—Clive Davis

In the early eighties the music business was experiencing a major decline which was only stemmed by the introduction of the CD format. This allowed companies with back-catalogue of interest to reissue old vinyl titles at great profit given that the format was being subsidized by reduced artist royalties, if indeed these re-issues bore royalties at all. It was the musical equivalent of re-inventing the wheel.

—Andy Dodd

In my opinion, bootlegs were the greatest promotional tool ever invented. I think that people like Pete Townshend who saw the wisdom in bootlegs and encouraged people to bootleg them, I think that's smart! We never sold large enough quantities to hurt . . .

—*"Dub," an unidentified bootlegger*

The music industry is toast. It has been completely overtaken by events and can do nothing about it.

—*Shaun Fanning*

The composer, in my estimation, has been helped a great deal by the mechanical reproduction of music. Music is written to be heard, and any instrument that tends to help it to be heard more frequently and by greater numbers is advantageous to the person who writes it. . . . The radio and the phonograph are harmful to the extent that they bastardize music and give currency to a lot of cheap things. They are not harmful to the composer.

—*George Gershwin*

In an unguarded moment some months ago, I predicted that the public concert as we know it today would no longer exist a century hence, that its functions would have been entirely taken over by electronic media. It had not occurred to me that this statement represented a particularly radical pronouncement. Indeed, I regarded it almost as self-evident truth and, in any case, as defining only one of the peripheral effects occasioned by developments in the electronic age. But never has a statement of mine been so widely quoted—or so hotly disputed.

—*Glenn Gould*

At first glance, it seems audiences were drawn to online music because of the power of the free, but in reality the rush to online music came from digitized sound's ever-expanding power of liquidity. . . . It wasn't only that it was free; it was all the things you could do with it. Once music is digitized, new behaviors emerge. . . . With digitization, music went from being a noun, to a verb, once again.

—*Kevin Kelly*

The grand upset that music is now experiencing—the transformation that Napster signalled—is the shift from analog copies to digital copies. The industrial age was driven by analog copies; analog copies are perfect and cheap. The information age is driven by digital copies; digital copies are perfect, fluid and free.

—Kevin Kelly

Since the advent of the gramophone, and more particularly the wireless, music of a sort is everywhere and at every time; in the heavens, the lower parts of the earth, the mountains, the forest and every tree therein. It is a Psalmist's nightmare.

—Constant Lambert

In the 1960s, the record companies seemed to sign anything with long hair; if it was a sheepdog, so what.

—Nick Mason

Music is spiritual. The music business is not.

—Van Morrison

To me, the music industry has got about as much meaning as a comic book.

—Van Morrison

I have always believed that the *sound* aspect of recordings was by far the least important. Otherwise we wouldn't have "Louie Louie."

—Todd Rundgren

All record companies prefer third-rate talents to true genius because they can push them around more easily, make them change their clothes or their politics just to sell more records.

—Nina Simone

If his packaging is simple, [a bootlegger] may be able to produce a small edition of a two-disc opera for as little as $1,000 to $1,500, and if he sells 100 or 150 copies at $10 he breaks even. The break-even point for a commercial company is 5,000 or 6,000 copies. Thus, a pirate or privateer can afford to issue connoisseur repertoire that would be financially disastrous for a major company.

—Stereo Review, *1970*

Free music, or almost free music, sounds sweet to me too. But if record companies are destroyed by the "new economics," and all artists offer their wares directly through the Web, I predict we will then discover that we have lost a crucial function we never gave record companies credit for: winnowing. With the demise of business as usual, every garage band in existence will have equal standing in the undifferentiated mass of millions of titles thrown up on the Web. Yes, downloads will be inexpensive, but how will one find the good stuff? Then we'll belatedly realize that those demonized record companies once had saved us from ourselves.

—Randall E. Stross

I can only say that I am astonished and somewhat terrified at the result of this evening's experiment. Astonished at the wonderful form you have developed and terrified at the thought that so much hideous and bad music will be put on record for ever.

—Arthur Sullivan, in a letter to Thomas Edison

Good, soulful songs that resonate in your emotional life are what it's all about. The delivery system's going to change, but in the end, what's the difference between AM radio and MP2. It really doesn't matter.

—Don Was

When you get in the music business, someone's gonna rip you anyway so that don't bother me.

—Muddy Waters

Reporters and Reporting

Reporters are like alligators. You don't have to love them; you don't necessarily have to like them. But you do have to feed them.

—*Anonymous White House source*

The plain truth is that the reporter's trade is for young men. Your feet, which do the legwork, are nine times more important than your head, which fits the facts into a coherent pattern.

—*Joseph Alsop*

Trying to be a first rate reporter on the average American newspaper is like trying to play Bach's St. Matthew Passion on a ukelele. The instrument is too crude for the work, for the audience and for the performer.

—*Ben H. Bagdikian*

Tell those guys out there to get the smell of warm blood into their copy.

—*Hugh Baillie*

We "muckraked" not because we hated our world but because we loved it.

—*Ray S. Baker*

As a kid, I did a lot of squirrel hunting. The trick was not to look for squirrels but to look for movement in the trees or in the bushes. That's what I do as a reporter. I watch for what's different.

—*Roger Charles*

The bad habits of what I call "know-it-all" reporting have become so ingrained that many of us have actually begun thinking of them as principles. . . . Civic journalism is, in part, an attempt to replace these bad habits with what are really nothing more than the basics of good reporting: shoe leather, a decent respect for the opinions of others, and a commitment to provide citizens with the information they need to meet the obligations of their citizenship.

—*Stan Cloud*

Never know a public man well enough that he inhibits you from writing about him frankly and fully while he's living his public life.

—*Alistair Cooke*

Each time a shoddy job of reporting is done by anyone, it hurts us all.

—*John Curley*

As James Reston has said, today's reporter is forced to become an educator more concerned with explaining the news than with being the first on the scene.

—*Fred Friendly*

Except [for] the Flood, nothing was ever as bad as reported.

—*E. W. Howe*

Guidelines for journalists working in Latin America:

If authorities can't guarantee you safety, get out of the country.
Never carry a gun or other weapon . . .
Resist abuse by authorities and always protest such abuse

of yourself and other professionals. But don't become
abusive yourself . . .
Avoid reporting from both sides of a conflict. Crossing
from one to the other is often dangerous.
Always carry a white flag.
Never point your finger; it may be mistaken for a gun.
Never wash your car. Tampering can be detected easily
on a dirty car.
If guerrillas at roadblocks ask you for a "war tax," give
something.

—Inter-American Press Association

I keep six honest serving-men
(They taught me all I knew);
Their names are What and Why and When
And How and Where and Who.

—Rudyard Kipling

Good reporting is to an event what a good map is to a city: It
reduces the original in size and accessibility while remaining
faithful to the basic features of the original. To simply train a
camera on a complicated event is not journalism, any more
than taking someone out on a boat and showing them a stretch
of coastline is cartography.

—Ted Koppel

Reporting by and large is being interested in everyone you
meet.

—A. J. Liebling

A biased journalist will lose credibility and sources, and when
you're without credibility and sources, you're not a reporter.

—John Mashek

Reporters are like blackbirds sitting on a telephone wire. One
flies off and they all fly off. One flies back and they all fly back.

—Eugene J. McCarthy

News stories work best when the writer has the skill to get out of the way and allow the reader to meet and hear the people in the story.

—Don Murray

I operate by a sense of smell. If something smells wrong, I go to work.

—Drew Pearson

We [reporters] huddle together for warmth too often. We should be less afraid to go out into the cold, all by ourselves.

—James Perry

The Khomeini Corollary: Take the revolution to where the reporters want to be and you'll get worldwide coverage.

—Charles Peters

Reporters are addressed as "Gentlemen of the Press" in the vain hope that they will behave as such, rather than as a statement of fact.

—Gerald Priestland

Never trust a reporter who has a nice smile.

—William Rauch

There aren't any embarrassing questions—just embarrassing answers.

—Carl Rowan

Report me and my cause aright.

—William Shakespeare, Hamlet

When I was a young reporter, the great vice was whiskey. Now the great vice is cynicism.

—Paul Simon, former U.S. Senator from Illinois

Reporter: Something between a whore and a bartender.

—*Wallace Smith*

He is someone who flies around from hotel to hotel and thinks the most interesting thing about any story is the fact that he has arrived to cover it.

—*Tom Stoppard,* Night and Day,
referring to a foreign correspondent

Reporting is the best school in the world to get a knowledge of human beings and human ways.

—*Mark Twain*

There are stories everywhere, if you can guide your feet there.

—*Ugandan journalism student*

I can get a better grasp of what is going on in the world from one good Washington dinner party than from all the background information NBC piles on my desk.

—*Barbara Walters*

Investigative reporters have the bias of piranha fish—they will go after anything that bleeds.

—*Ben J. Wattenberg*

When a reporter sits down at the typewriter, he's nobody's friend.

—*Theodore H. White*

See also *Journalism; Journalists; Sources and Subjects*

Sources and Subjects

The reporter has to talk to enough people so that he can reduce the degree to which he is misled.

—Joseph and Stewart Alsop

Whenever people get a choice between privacy and accountability, they tend to choose privacy for themselves and accountability for everyone else.

—David Brin

When talking to the press remember they always have the last word.

—H. Jackson Brown Jr.

The only thing worse than being misquoted is not being quoted at all.

—Willie Brown, San Francisco mayor

Twenty-five years in Washington has taught me never to tell a lie to a reporter.

—Joseph A. Califano Jr.

The reporter is in a position of supplicant. You—the source— have something he wants: information. But if you, as an official, look at it only that way, then you're in trouble because he also has something you want: access to the public. And it's important to remember that reporters also provide sources with a conduit enabling them to get their messages across to their adversaries and their allies.

—Hodding Carter

"No comment" is a splendid expression. I am using it again and again.

—Winston Churchill

As individuals reporters can take advantage of their humanity, suffer with the victim, participate in and facilitate a process of catharsis and grief, and help give public meaning to the life of the victim. The problem occurs when the journalist becomes part of an anonymous and rapacious group. . . . It is the public vision of the voracious, unfeeling pack that dehumanizes us, hurts victims, and makes us so unpopular.

—Roy Peter Clark

If you want something to remain off the record, don't say it.

—Anita Creamer

Don't quote what I said, quote what I mean.

—Richard J. Daley, Chicago mayor

When you're talking to the media, be a well, not a fountain.

—Michael Deaver

The press is savage. It doesn't forgive anything. They only track the mistakes. Each intention is misread, every gesture criticized.

—Princess Diana, the week before her death

The problem of journalism in America proceeds from a simple but inescapable bind: journalists are rarely, if ever, in a position to establish the truth about an issue for themselves, and they are therefore almost entirely dependent on self-interested "sources" for the version of reality that they report.

—Edward Jay Epstein

The number of errors in any piece of writing rises in proportion to the writer's reliance on secondary sources.

—Harold Faber

I'm the guy they call Deep Throat.

—Mark Felt, legendary Watergate source

One of the strengths of the press is that our reporters can talk with people that government investigators often cannot or will not consult; they give us information only if we keep their identities confidential. Their status in the community, their careers, perhaps even their lives might otherwise be in jeopardy. When we accept the conditions of confidentiality, it is a sacred trust. We decide that the information is more important than the identity of the provider.

—Gene Foreman

Beware anonymous sources. They can lie without accountability. They can fudge without responsibility. They can hide behind anonymity. They can strain readers' credulity and damage journalists' credibility.

—Michael Gartner

The freedom of the press works in such a way that there is not much freedom from it.

—Princess Grace of Monaco

The "media" in their long history have shattered countless reputations and destroyed countless careers. We have driven people to suicide. We have caused immeasurable emotional pain, suffering and humiliation, not only to individuals but to families . . . and to entire communities.

—Richard Harwood

I notice that in spite of the frightful lies you have printed about me I still believe everything you print about other people.

—*Robert Maynard Hutchins*

I want the truth; *they* want to be beautiful.

—*Thomas Morgan*

Looking at yourself through the media is like looking at one of those rippled mirrors in an amusement park.

—*Edmund S. Muskie*

Nobody believes the official spokesman but everybody trusts an unidentified source.

—*Ron Nessen*

The use of unnamed sources is among American newspapers' most damaging habits.

—*Geneva Overholser*

Anonymous sources play the press as if it were their own private troupe of puppeteers.

—*Peter S. Prichard*

Regular people are not equipped to deal with the viciousness of the media.

—*Marilyn Quayle*

In dealing with the press, do yourself a favor, stick with one of three responses: (a) I know and I can tell you; (b) I know and I can't tell you; (c) I don't know.

—*Dan Rather*

Wednesday . . . marked *New York Times* reporter Judith Miller's sixth week in jail for *not* writing about an undercover CIA officer and *not* saying whom she talked to about the story she didn't write. It has been 109 weeks since Robert

Novak, the conservative Chicago columnist who *did* write a column identifying Valerie Plame as a CIA officer, got away with apparently breaking the law. It has been even longer since [White House official] Karl Rove discussed the [identify of the] operative with the media and—so far—has gotten away with it. . . . On Monday, Miller will have spent more time in jail than any other reporter for an American media outlet in modern history. That will surpass William Farr, . . . jailed in 1972 for 46 days for not revealing sources in a criminal proceeding. . . . That milestone should not pass lightly.

—Rochelle Riley, August 19, 2005

The stickiest problem in journalism is defining the proper stance of the reporter toward his source.

—William Rivers

People love the unvarnished truth if it's about others, and hate it when it's about themselves.

—Warren Rogers

[Journalists] don't take pictures or gather information and then trade it with the police or trade it with prosecutors. They don't do things like that, because, if they did, they would never get the interviews from whistleblowers, from watchdogs on government, from people who want to share information with them but who are terribly afraid of retribution by the government.

—Bruce W. Sanford

I'm sure if I have any plans, the press will inform me.

—Arthur Scargill, British trade union leader

[The Judy Miller] case was never about protecting government sources who risk their careers by telling the truth, but rather about punishing those like [Joseph C.] Wilson who do. That Miller cared far more about protecting someone who abused his power as the vice president's chief of staff than about protecting the right of Wilson to speak truth to power says volumes about her priorities.

—*Robert Scheer*

I feel that I have been victimized. There's nobody out there checking on the media.

—*O. J. Simpson*

She [Princess Diana] talked endlessly of getting away from England, mainly because of the treatment she received at the hands of the newspapers. I don't think she ever understood why her genuinely good intentions were sneered at by the media, why there appeared to be a permanent quest on their behalf to bring her down. It is baffling. My own, and only, explanation is that genuine goodness is threatening to those at the opposite end of the moral spectrum.

—*Earl Spencer, Princess Diana's brother*

Facing the press is more difficult than bathing a leper.

—*Mother Teresa*

Journalists are as disruptive a menace to the public body as stones in the gall bladder are to the private body. They are the scavengers of society who, possessing no guts of their own, tear out the guts of celebrities.

—*Caitlin Thomas, widow of poet Dylan Thomas*

From the standpoint of the State Department, the White House, [and] the Pentagon, the press is looked on as a dangerous, unattractive beast, which you can lead along for a little bit of the way, but which is likely to turn and bite you at the slightest opportunity.

—*Unidentified State Department official*

Publish and be damned.

—*The Duke of Wellington, (attributed), supposedly his response to a blackmailing letter from a publisher*

Journalists are not your friends. It's not that reporters aren't decent people—they are. They are not interviewing you to meet a new friend, but to get a story. Their job always comes first and don't forget it.

—*Robert L. Woodrum*

Look at all the stuff that's been from anonymous sources over the years and very little of it has been wrong. In fact, I would argue it's often more correct because the reporter knows his or her rear end is on the line.

—*Bob Woodward*

See also *Credibility, Accuracy and Bias; Photography; Readers; Reporters*

Sports

Let's face it, sports writers, we're not hanging around with brain surgeons.

—Jimmy Cannon

What's the difference between a three-week-old puppy and a sportswriter? In six weeks, the puppy stops whining.

—Mike Ditka

The capacity of sporting journalists to wax lyrical in the face of the exceptional is matched only by the speed with which they run out of adjectives in doing so.

—Derek Malcolm

If you guys could get just one percent of the stories right.

—John McEnroe, U.S. tennis player

My job is to coach; yours is to write. If we can't work hand in glove, then there is something wrong with our professions.

—Lou Little, to a group of sportswriters

These are games we are dealing with, not Armageddon.

—Joe McGuff

There is more action and movement in sportswriting than there is in writing news.

—Grantland Rice

Needless to say, the reporter should be treated as a gentleman. A great many of the misunderstandings between coaches and the press are caused by an attitude of hostility by both. But as a coach you should remember that when you talk to a reporter, you are talking to your public.

—Don Scannell

I once thought of becoming a political cartoonist because they only have to come up with one idea a day. Then I thought I'd become a sportswriter instead, because they don't have to come up with any.

—Sam Snead

If I ever needed a brain transplant, I'd choose a sportswriter because I'd want a brain that had never been used.

—Norm van Brocklin

I always turn to the sports section first. The sports page records people's accomplishments; the front page has nothing but man's failures.

—Earl Warren

[College basketball players] are going to meet a lot of weirdos in the real world, so why not let them talk to the press?

—Gary Williams, basketball coach

Tabloids

A newspaper for those who move their lips when they look at pictures.

—Anonymous

Tabloid: A scream-lined newspaper.

—Anonymous

On the whole the British don't believe what they read in their tabloids. They trust the sports pages; the rest is assumed to be saucy nonsense, lightly seasoned with souped-up fact.

—Neal Ascherson

Supermarket tabloids virtually define the word "trash"— sensational, excessive, gossipy, stereotyped. They are so unvalued that they are completely ephemeral; loyal readers may keep favorite issues and stories, but libraries shun them. While critics often call them sleazy, sexy or immoral, the papers in fact cast themselves as guardians of a particular kind of moral code that sits well with their regular readers.

—S. Elizabeth Bird

A good "Hey, Martha" would be a story about a body discovered with no wounds and an autopsy revealing no human heart. Or a story about a six-month-old Chinese baby who can accurately describe the physical layout of the Malden, MA, public library. Something very weird but compelling. To have

The Boss tell you that a story of yours is a "Hey, Martha" is the local equivalent of winning a Pulitzer Prize.

—*P. J. Corkery, tabloid journalist*

It's wonderful. I love talking to witches and Satanists and vampire hunters, and people who've been kidnapped by UFOs—it sure beats covering zoning board meetings.

—*Cliff Linedecker*

If we're worried about an erosion of public trust and the tabloidization of our values, how likely is it that a line is going to be drawn anywhere between us and supermarket tabloids if we don't say collectively, "We do some things and we don't do other things"?

—*Robin MacNeil*

Five things. Violence. Sex. Blood—no, that doesn't count. Money. Kids. Animals. Is that five?

—*Mike Pearl,* New York Post *editor*
listing the elements that make a tabloid

I watched a wild hog eat my baby!

—*Bill Sloan, title of his history of tabloid journalism*

Technology and the Media

The Information Age could leave us with no information at all, only assertions.

—Joel Achenbach

In guessing the direction of technology it is wise to ask who is in the best position to profit most.

—Ben H. Bagdikian

It's not hard to slip from cyberspace to cyberchaos.

—Louis D. Boccardi

[The telegraph] binds together by a vital cord all the nations of the earth. It is impossible that old prejudices and hostilities should longer exist, while such an instrument has been created for an exchange of thought between all the nations of the earth.

—Charles Briggs and Augustus Maverick, 1858

A memex is a device in which an individual stores all his books, records, and communications, and which is mechanized so that it may be consulted with exceeding speed and flexibility. It is an enlarged intimate supplement to his memory.

—Vannevar Bush, 1945

If you think of all the innovations, the successful ones, in communications and the media in virtually our lifetime—all of them have been based on someone's insight that went contrary to the information available at the moment.

—Richard Clurman

No matter how many calendars we keep, how many lists we make, how fast we clear our literal or figurative desktops, how upgraded our central processing units and modems, how many channels we get, how many Napster downloads we perform— or perhaps precisely because of all these calendars, lists, desktops, channels and downloads—we cannot, cannot possibly keep up.

—Todd Gitlin

[N]o matter what kind of machine you have, no matter what color it is, how pretty it is, how fast it works, if you have nothing to say to your reader, who cares?

—Erwin Jaffe

A journalist who can't read a reel of magnetic tape is as illiterate as the fifteenth century peasant confronted by Gutenberg.

—Elliot Jaspin

The capacity to "go live" also creates its own terrible dynamic. Much, if not most, of the process of good journalism lies in the evaluation, the assessment, the *editing* of raw material. Putting someone on the air while an event is unfolding is clearly a technological tour de force—but it is an impediment, not an aid, to good journalism.

—Ted Koppel

You cannot endow even the best machine with initiative; the jolliest steamroller will not plant flowers.

—Walter Lippmann

Gutenberg makes everybody a reader. Xerox makes everybody a publisher.

—Marshall McLuhan

The new electronic interdependence recreates the world in the image of a global village.

—Marshall McLuhan

There is a basic principle that distinguishes a hot medium like radio from a cool one like the telephone, or a hot medium like the movie from a cool one like TV. A hot medium is one that extends one single sense in "high definition." High definition is the state of being well filled with data. A photograph is, visually, "high definition." A cartoon is low definition simply because very little visual information is provided. . . . Hot media are, therefore, low in participation, and cool media are high in participation or completion by the audience.

—Marshall McLuhan

We are today as far into the electronic age as the Elizabethans had advanced into the typographical and mechanical age. And we are experiencing the same confusions and indecisions which they had felt when living simultaneously in two contrasted forms of society and experience.

—Marshall McLuhan

Users of news and information won't change except there will be more of them. On-line will be when you want it and searchable. Telephone, TV, and on-line will converge slowly. There will be many more journalists and much more news. Verifying facts and sources will be harder on-line—a new responsibility for journalists.

—Robert Metcalfe

The digital era admittedly has caused some of us a bit of uncertainty. Yet it must be looked upon as a blessing for newspapers. It provides access to a medium without government licensing or regulation and with two things we have always wanted: immediacy and more space.

—William S. Morris III

What hath God wrought?

> —*Samuel F. B. Morse, first official*
> *telegraph message, 1844*

My God, it talks!

> —*Pedro II, emperor of Brazil, (attributed),*
> *on hearing a telephone in the U.S. in 1876*

When wires, radio waves, satellites and computers became major vehicles of discourse, regulation seemed to be a technical necessity. And so, as speech increasingly flows over these electronic media, the five-century growth of an unabridged right of citizens to speak without controls may be endangered.

> —*Ithiel de Sola Pool*

There are newspapers whose editors do not yet grasp that in a technological world information is a problem, not a solution.

> —*Neil Postman*

The United States enjoys an inbuilt national predilection for new technology, partly fostered by newspapers and journalism. It was hardly surprising that the industry was attracted to its own mythology.

> —*Anthony Smith*

Satellites and microwave relay stations give reporters the power to make or destroy lives in a nanosecond: One moment a politician is behaving like an imbecile, the next moment everyone in the world is watching it on the tube.

> —*Tony Snow*

I have always wished that my computer would be as easy to use as my telephone. My wish has come true. I no longer know how to use my telephone.

> —*Bjarne Stroustrup, computer scientist*

It may be that "interactive television" for most viewers might turn out to be an oxymoron. . . . Millions of American already spend much of their day interacting with a keyboard and a screen; will they really want to do more of this once they get home?

—Robert Thompson

But what if Maine and Texas have nothing to communicate?
—Henry David Thoreau, on learning that
these states had been linked by telegraph

At the beginning of the 21st century six new technologies— micro-electronics, computers, telecommunications, new man-made materials, robotics, and biotechnology—are interacting to create a new and very different economic world.

—Lester Thurow

I believe that composing on the typewriter has probably done more than anything else to deteriorate English prose.

—Edmund Wilson

Television

TV—a clever contraption derived from the words Terrible Vaudeville—we call it a medium because nothing's well done.

—*Goodman Ace*

Is it not fair and relevant to question its [the power of television] concentration in the hands of a tiny and closed fraternity of privileged men, elected by no one, and enjoying a monopoly sanctioned and licensed by government?

—*Spiro Agnew*

A device that permits people who haven't anything to do to watch people who can't do anything.

—*Fred Allen*

The triumph of machinery over people.

—*Fred Allen*

In California they don't throw their garbage away—they make it into TV shows.

—*Woody Allen*

Appearing on TV is becoming its own political end: I blink, therefore I am; I'm perky, therefore I help people. This is a world where "communicating" is more important than what you communicate, where words are mistaken for deeds and images magically transformed into accomplishments.

—*Jonathan Alter*

Everybody is an authority on television.

—*Anonymous*

The human race is faced with a cruel choice: work or daytime television.

—*Anonymous*

The titillated masses scramble aboard this pre-routed cattle car that transports them into an intellectual Auschwitz.

—*Anonymous*

Every civilization creates its own cultural garbage and ours is television.

—*Michael Arlen*

In 1927 Philo T. Farnsworth transmitted television images without wires. . . . Farnsworth used the dollar sign as a test pattern.

—*Ben H. Bagdikian*

Televisio ergo sum—I am televised, therefore I am.

—*Russell Baker*

Christian television is basically very boring.

—*Tammy Faye Bakker*

Television is the first truly democratic culture—the first culture available to everybody and entirely governed by what the people want. The most terrifying thing is what the people do want.

—*Clive Barnes*

In its brief history television has become the American people's most important source of ideas, apart from interpersonal contact.

—*Leo Bogart*

Do you realize that if it weren't for Edison we'd be watching TV by candlelight?

—*Al Boliska*

Nothing is "really" real unless it happens on television.

—*Daniel J. Boorstin*

The television, that insidious beast, that Medusa which freezes a billion people to stone every night, staring fixedly, that Siren which called and sang and promised so much and gave, after all, so little.

—*Ray Bradbury*

[Television] has recreated for the great democracies one of the conditions of the Greek city-state: all citizens can see and hear their leaders.

—*Lord Brain*

People who deny themselves television deny themselves participation in life today. They are self-exiled from the world.

—*John Mason Brown*

Unlike productions in the other arts, all television shows are born to destroy two other shows.

—*Les Brown*

The best that can be said for Norwegian television is that it gives you the sensation of a coma without the worry and inconvenience.

—*Bill Bryson*

Television has a real problem. They have no page two.

—*Art Buchwald*

I've never seen it chiselled on stone tablets that TV must be uplifting.

—*Johnny Carson*

Strangers often come up to me and say, "I saw you on television." To them it's a sort of confirmation that I exist.

—Hugh Casson

As long as people will accept crap, it will be financially profitable to dispense it.

—Dick Cavett

Television is not the truth. . . . We lie like hell. . . . We deal in illusions, man. None of it is true. But you people sit there day after day, night after night. . . . We're all you know. You're beginning to believe the illusions we're spinning here. You're beginning to think that the tube is reality and that your own lives are like the tube, you eat like the tube, you raise your children like the tube. This is mass madness, you maniacs. In God's name, you people are the real thing. We are the illusion. So turn off your television sets. Turn them off right now.

—Paddy Chayefsky, creator of the TV anchor
Howard Beale, in the movie Network

Television is more interesting than people. If it were not, we should have people standing in the corners of our rooms.

—Alan Coren

The vast wasteland of TV is not interested in producing a better mousetrap but in producing a worse mouse.

—Laurence C. Coughlin

Television thrives on unreason and unreason thrives on television. It strikes at the emotions rather than the intellect.

—Robin Day

You have debased [my] child. . . . You have made him a laughingstock of intelligence . . . a stench in the nostrils of the gods of the ionosphere.

—Lee De Forest, one of TV's inventors

While theoretically and technically television may be feasible, commercially and financially I consider it an impossibility, a development of which we need waste little time dreaming.

—Lee De Forest, 1926

Any entertainment program, no matter how bad, will drive out any public affairs program, no matter how good.

—Edwin Diamond

Television is a medium of entertainment which permits millions of people to listen to the same joke at the same time, and yet remain lonesome.

—T. S. Eliot

Television is a gift of God, and God will hold those who utilize his divine instrument accountable to Him.

—Philo T. Farnsworth

MTV is the lava lamp of the 1980s.

—Doug Ferrari

Because television can make so much money doing its worst, it often cannot afford to do its best.

—Fred Friendly

The sound bite, which has become so pervasive in political fisticuffs, is to the First Amendment as bumper stickers are to philosophy.

—John E. Frohnmayer

Television is an invention that permits you to be entertained in your living room by people you wouldn't have in your home.

—David Frost

Television: The third parent.

—R. Buckminster Fuller

Television

Why should people go out and pay money to see bad films when they can stay at home and see bad television for nothing?

—Sam Goldwyn

TV Commercial: The last refuge of optimism in a world of gloom.

—Cedric Hardwicke

In the age of television, image becomes more important than substance.

—S. I. Hayakawa

We can put television in its proper light by supposing that Gutenberg's great invention had been directed at printing only comic books.

—Robert Maynard Hutchins

Television is simultaneously blamed, often by the same people, for worsening the world and for being powerless to change it.

—Clive James

All television is educational television. The only question is what is it teaching?

—Nicholas Johnson

The difference between ordinary television and cable is the difference between a garden hose and Niagara Falls.

—Nicholas Johnson

We are drowning our youngsters in violence, cynicism and sadism piped into the living room and even the nursery. The grandchildren of the kids who used to weep because the Little Match Girl froze to death now feel cheated if she isn't slugged, raped and thrown into a Bessemer converter.

—Jenkin Lloyd Jones

Capitalism isn't just an unjust economic system. It's a way of life that leads to a corruption of important values. Television is only one example.

—Nikita S. Khrushchev

Suppose someone invented an instrument, a convenient little talking tube, say, which could be heard over the whole land. I wonder if the police would not forbid it, fearing that the whole country would become mentally deranged if it were used.

—Sören Kierkegaard

Pure drivel tends to drive ordinary drivel off the TV screen.

—Marvin Kitman

Television: An instrument of intense pressure that convinces the immature mind that violence is an accepted way of life. It is a subtle form of American brainwashing. The fatal consequences will be known by posterity. . . . Exposing children to such violence can be compared with taking children to public tortures and hangings in medieval times.

—Frank J. Kronenberg

Television has proved that people will look at anything rather than each other.

—Ann Landers

Educational television should be absolutely forbidden. It can only lead to unreasonable disappointment when your child discovers that the letters of the alphabet do not leap up out of books and dance around with royal-blue chickens.

—Fran Lebowitz

Television is like a gold [sic] goose that lays scrambled eggs; and it is futile and probably fatal to beat it for not laying caviar. Anyway, more people like scrambled eggs than caviar.

—Lee Loevinger

Television is the literature of the illiterate, the culture of the low-brow, the wealth of the poor, the privilege of the under-privileged, the exclusive club of the excluded masses.

—Lee Loevinger

The cable TV sex channels don't expand our horizons, don't make us better people, and don't come in clearly enough.

—Bill Maher

Television pollutes identity.

—Norman Mailer

If the television craze continues with the present level of pro-grams, we are destined to have a nation of morons.

—Daniel Marsh, 1950

I find television very educating. Every time somebody turns on the set I go into the other room and read a book.

—Groucho Marx

The TV thing itself is very, very polluting. It goes right into the nervous system. . . . To the ordinary kid without a lot of literacy, TV will just turn off any possibility of left hemisphere. It's like, for example, booze. Nonliterate societies cannot touch it. They just go berserk . . .

—Marshall McLuhan

Thanks to television, for the first time the young are seeing history made before it is censored by their elders.

—Margaret Mead

Television exposes kids to behavior that adults spent centuries trying to hide from children.

—Joshua Meyerowitz

Everyone watches television. But no one really likes it.

—Mark C. Miller

Children will watch anything, and when a broadcaster uses crime and violence and other shoddy devices to monopolize a child's attention it's worse than taking candy from a baby. It is taking precious time from the process of growing up.

—Newton Minow

In 1961 I worried that my children would not benefit much from television, but in 1991 I worry that my grandchildren will actually be harmed by it.

—Newton Minow

On a par with the atomic bomb, television is the most important invention of our century.

—Newton Minow

When television is good, nothing—not the theater, not the magazines or newspapers—nothing is better. But when television is bad, nothing is worse. I invite you to sit down in front of your television set when your station goes on the air and stay there without a book, magazine, newspaper, profit-and-loss sheet, or rating book to distract you, and keep your eyes glued to that set until the station signs off. I can assure you that you will observe a vast wasteland.

—Newton Minow, May 10, 1961

I maintain that there is now more good television available than there is time to watch. But, if you looked at it all, you'd be a passive spectator of life, not a participant . . . the trick is to be selective. Choose carefully from among what is available. Good television does what a good book does—spurs the imagination and creates images in your mind that compel you, the individual, to cross boundaries that have psychological "no trespassing" signs on them. That happens when you have good television.

—Bill Moyers

As a television performer, I see myself as a man playing a piano in a brothel, who includes [the hymn] "Abide With Me" in his repertoire in the hope of thereby edifying both clients and inmates.

—Malcolm Muggeridge

I have had my [TV] aerials removed—it's the moral equivalent of a prostate operation.

—Malcolm Muggeridge

Television was not intended to make human beings vacuous, but it is an emanation of their vacuity.

—Malcolm Muggeridge

I would like television to produce some itching pills, rather than this endless outpouring of tranquilizers.

—Edward R. Murrow

Just because you speak in a voice loud enough to be heard over television by 16 million people, that doesn't make you any smarter than you were when you spoke loudly enough to be heard only at the other end of the bar.

—Edward R. Murrow (attributed)

The actions of the junior Senator from Wisconsin have caused alarm and dismay among our allies abroad and given considerable comfort to our enemies, and whose fault is that? Not really his. He didn't create this situation of fear; he merely exploited it, and rather successfully. Cassius was right: "The fault, dear Brutus, is not in our stars but in ourselves. . . ." Good night, and good luck.

—Edward R. Murrow, "See it Now" broadcast on Sen. Joe McCarthy, March 9, 1954

This instrument can teach, it can illuminate, it can even inspire, but only if human being are willing to use it to those ends. Otherwise it is only wires and lights in a box.

—Edward R. Murrow

One reason that children are inclined to learn from television is that it . . . is never too busy to talk to them, and it never has to brush them aside while it does household chores. . . . Television seems to want their attention at any time, and goes to considerable lengths to attract it.

*—National Commission on Causes
and Prevention of Violence, 1969*

I think television ruins everything it touches.

—Ron Nessen

The American people don't believe anything until they see it on television.

—Richard M. Nixon

Dictum on television scripts: We don't want it good—we want it Tuesday.

—Dennis Norden

[T]he trend toward larger and larger televisions will continue as screens continue to double in size every 18 months. Televisions will eventually grow so large that families will be forced to watch them outside their homes, peering in through the window. Random wolf attacks will make viewing more dangerous.

—Conan O'Brien

Yet, while getting bigger and more pervasive, and periodically laying claim to accomplishments of unquestioned value and stature, the television landscape remains essentially and distressingly the same as that described by Minow. Substitute "disease of the week" movies for the westerns, and the picture is still all too familiar. As one analyst after another has pointed out over the decades, commercial television is in the business not of creating programs but of supplying audiences to advertisers who generally do not want their potential customers to be unduly upset.

—John J. O'Connor

Television lies. All television lies. It lies persistently, instinctively and by habit. . . . A culture of mendacity surrounds the medium, and those who work there live in it, breathe it and prosper by it. . . . I know of no area of public life—no, not even politics—more saturated by professional cynicism.

—Matthew Parris

When I was young we didn't have MTV; we had to take drugs and go to concerts.

—Steven Pearl

Peter's Television Law: If it moves, the public will watch it.

—Laurence Peter

Unless and until there is unmistakable proof to the contrary, the presumption must be that television is and will be a main factor in influencing the values and moral standards of our society. . . . Television does not, and cannot, merely reflect the moral standards of society. It must affect them, either by changing or by reinforcing them.

—Pilkington Report, Great Britain, 1960

My mother didn't allow our family to have a television because she said it contributed to mind rot.

—Janet Reno

Television is the bland leading the bland.

—Murray Schumach

Television? The word is half Latin and half Greek. No good can come of it.

—C. P. Scott

Men don't care what's on TV. They only care what else is on TV.

—Jerry Seinfeld (attributed)

How do you put on a meaningful drama or documentary that is adult, incisive, probing when every fifteen minutes the proceedings are interrupted by twelve dancing rabbits with toilet paper?

—Rod Serling

TV cameras are our modern-day witches. See how they have transformed witnesses into babbling tabloid stars, judges into fops, victims into fools and lawyers into shysters. "Cameraitis" is a deadly disease. Most never recover from it.

—Gerry Spence

The standards in television have gone to an all-time low, and I'm here to represent the change.

—Howard Stern

If you read a lot of books, you're considered well-read. But if you watched a lot of TV, you're not considered well-viewed.

—Lily Tomlin

He . . . told me that the show was merely entertainment and that giving help to quiz contestants was a common practice and merely a part of show business. This of course was not true, but perhaps I wanted to believe him.

—Charles Van Doren, testifying how the producer of the quiz show Twenty One gave him answers in advance

There are days when any electrical appliance in the house, including the vacuum cleaner, seems to offer more entertainment possibilities than the TV set.

> —*Harriet van Horne*

I'm always amazed that people will actually choose to sit in front of the television and just be savaged by stuff that belittles their intelligence.

> —*Alice Walker*

I hate television. I hate it as much as peanuts. But I can't stop eating peanuts.

> —*Orson Welles*

He who is created by television can be destroyed by television.

> —*Theodore H. White*

Getting an award from TV is like getting kissed by someone with bad breath.

> —*Mason Williams*

In television you don't have to fake real life.

> —*Oprah Winfrey*

[Television] Chewing gum for the eyes.

> —*Frank Lloyd Wright (attributed);*
> *also attributed to John Mason Brown*

Television won't be able to hold onto any market it captures after the first six months. People will soon get tired of staring at a plywood box every night.

> —*Darryl F. Zanuck*

See also *Broadcasting; Television News*

Television News

To the top executives of these [TV network] giants, the news operation looks more and more like a box somewhere out on the edge of the organization chart—a box whose occupants add less than their share to the bottom line and, if left to their own devices, have an annoying tendency to emit rude noises.

—*Ken Auletta*

There is a bias in television journalism. It is not against any particular party or point of view—it is a bias against *understanding*.

—*John Birt*

The one function that TV news performs very well is that when there is no news we give it to you with the same emphasis as if there were.

—*David Brinkley*

We don't just have egg on our face. We have omelette all over our suits.

—*Tom Brokaw, on the TV networks' premature announcement that Al Gore won the 2000 presidential election*

Don't be quick to want to get on the air and anchor. Learn to write. If you write well, you can do anything in this business.

—*Connie Chung*

And that's the way it is.
> —*Walter Cronkite, CBS Evening News sign-off*

In Dallas, Texas, three shots were fired at President Kennedy's motorcade. The first reports say the President was "seriously· wounded."
> —*Walter Cronkite, Nov. 22, 1963*

There was a first wave of nausea, the sickening sensation that we were going under, that all of our efforts to hold network television news aloof from show business had failed.
> —*Walter Cronkite*

[Broadcast journalists] feel the wash of an accelerating tide away from news business and toward just plain show business. News divisions, which once may have enjoyed some kind of special standing within their companies, may now be perceived as just another chicken in the corporate hothouse, to be stuffed or starved as may serve the corporate purpose.
> —*Osborn Elliott*

There is no reason to confuse television news with journalism.
> —*Nora Ephron*

The printed press does not show the reporter asking the question. What is peculiar to television is that the intrusiveness is part of the story.
> —*Reuven Frank*

I am resigning [as head of CBS news] because CBS News did not carry the Senate foreign relations hearings [on the Vietnam war] last Thursday. . . . I am resigning because the decision not to carry the hearings made a mockery of the Paley-Stanton Columbia News division crusade of many years that demands access to congressional debate. . . . We cannot, in our public utterances, demand such access and then, in one of the crucial debates of our time, abdicate that responsibility . . .

—Fred Friendly

The news is the one thing networks can point to with pride. Everything else they do is crap, and they know it.

—Fred Friendly

"Katrinagate" was public service journalism ruthlessly exposing the truth on a live and continuous basis. Instead of secretive "Deep Throat" meetings in car-parks, cameras captured the immediate reality of what was happening at the New Orleans Convention Center, making a mockery of the stalling and excuses being put forward by those in power. Amidst the horror, American broadcast journalism just might have grown its spine back, thanks to Katrina.

—Matt Wells Gordon

When there was a disaster, it used to be that people went to church and all held hands. . . . Now the minute anything happens they run to CNN.

—Don Hewitt

If you stop and really listen to how a typical television reporter tells a story, you'll hear how artificial it sounds. Even words— "pontiff" comes quickly to mind—that you never hear in real life. Nobody talks that way—except us.

—Andrew Heyward, President of CBS News

I think that CNN will be reporting from virtually all nations of the world to all nations of the world. We will do it not only in English but in many other languages.

—W. Thomas Johnson

If [television news] can be talking about the tragic loss of life . . . in one breath and switch in the next breath to a commercial for cockroach traps, what kind of intrinsic decorum does television really have anyway?

—*Hiroshi Kume*

Anyone who has intimations of fame or immortality chose the wrong career in TV news. This business is so fast and fleeting, I don't think anything lasts for very long.

—*Charles Kuralt*

If Jesus Christ reappeared on Earth and began to talk to the multitudes, TV would cut away from him for livelier pictures.

—*Robert MacNeil*

I'm pessimistic . . . because all the trends in television journalism are toward the sensational, the hype, the hyperactive, the tabloid values to drive out the serious.

—*Robert MacNeil*

There is a misunderstanding . . . that television [news] has to sound belligerent in order to be tough.

—*Robert MacNeil*

In a medium in which a news piece takes a minute and an "indepth" piece takes two minutes, the simple will drive out the complex.

—*Frank Mankiewicz*

What they really want is a red-nosed clown with a physics degree.

—*Ian McCaskill, British TV weatherman*
on the ideal requirements for his job

All you need to run a news division is common sense and a good deal of concern for humanity.

—*Edward R. Murrow*

One of the basic troubles with radio and television news is that both instruments have grown up as an incompatible combination of show business, advertising and news. Each of the three is a rather bizarre and demanding profession. And when you get all three under one roof, the dust never settles.

—*Edward R. Murrow*

Everywhere I went I saw anchorpersons—men and women—devoting the crucial 30 minutes immediately before air time not to gathering and writing the news, but to applying makeup on their faces and spraying their hair into immobility.

—*Ron Nessen*

You have in your hands the most sacred trust that CBS has. Your job is to keep CBS News holy—and I expect you to do it.

—*William Paley, head of CBS,*
to Fred Friendly, President of CBS News

"Eyewitless news" contains little in the way of useful information . . . of ongoing, integrated issues and concerns, of attempts to dig beneath the surface for more enduring truths and subtle shadings—a twinkie of the airwaves.

—*Ron Powers*

Anyone who says network news cannot be profitable doesn't know what he is talking about. But anyone who says it must *always* make money is misguided and irresponsible.

—*Dan Rather*

In city after city, the news is delivered by newsmen turned actors, very bad actors. They grin, they laugh, they chuckle or moan the news. . . . They kid each other or applaud each other. And any day now, one of them will sing the news while doing a buck-and-wing stark naked.

—*Eric Sevareid*

[Anchoring TV news is] only reading a teleprompter. I mean, they make it seem like it's journalism.

—Jerry Springer

Information is power. I see CNN as the democratization of information.

—Ted Turner

See, we're gonna take the news and put it on satellite and then we're gonna beam it down to Russia, and we're gonna bring world peace and we're gonna get rich in the process!

—Ted Turner, at the launch of CNN, 1980

Television is show business and thus TV news is a part of show business.

—Av Westin

See also *News; Television*

War and the Media

We in the press have been accused, often unfairly, of creating and influencing policy. . . . My honest opinion is that we do have an effect, sometimes negative and sometimes positive, but we cannot make policy unless there is a policy vacuum. As long as an administration does not have a coherent policy, then that vacuum will be filled by television pictures or newspaper stories or radio reports. But as long as they have a policy, then I think our influence is the right one.

—*Christiane Amanpour*

After more than 130 years, the fundamental dispute between the American media and the American military has changed hardly at all. The essential argument is still about access. How much should the press be allowed to know and see of the conduct of battle?

—*Peter Andrews*

At their worst the military wraps itself in the flag and the media wrap themselves in the First Amendment and neither party listens to the other.

—*Peter Andrews*

I was a sergeant in Vietnam and now I am a journalist here [in the Gulf war]. In both wars, I feel like I'm in the wrong place at the wrong time, and I am going to go home and have people throw rocks at me.

—*John Balzar*

TV people tend to forget [that] military operations are not staged for the purpose of entertaining large audiences.

—Peter Braestrup

In wartime, truth is so precious that she should always be attended by a bodyguard of lies.

—Winston Churchill

I, like every soldier of America, will die for the freedom of the press, even for the freedom of newspapers that call me everything that is a good deal less than being a gentleman.

—Dwight D. Eisenhower

The first essential in military operations is that no information of value shall be given to the enemy. The first essential in newspaper work and broadcasting is wide-open publicity. It is your job and mine to try to reconcile those sometimes diverse considerations.

—Dwight D. Eisenhower

The "Five O'clock Follies?" Oh, it was ludicrous. It was painful to see. Some briefer, a colonel, would get up there and you'd watch his trial by fire as reporters would taunt him. He was hardly responsible for the mess, but they gave such duplicitous information and figures, and after a while it was just part of the heavy sadness of it all. It was impossible even to laugh at them and their loony tunes.

*—Gloria Emerson, referring to press
briefings during the Vietnam War*

You furnish the pictures, I'll furnish the war.

*—William Randolph Hearst (attributed), supposedly in a
cable sent to Frederick Remington in Cuba on the eve
of the Spanish-American war, 1898; many journalism
historians now seriously doubt Hearst wrote this.*

241

The first casualty when war comes is truth.

—Hiram Johnson

In a time of war the nation is always of one mind, eager to hear something good of themselves, and ill of the enemy. At this time the task of news writers is easy.

—Samuel Johnson

Much of the excitement of covering the [Gulf] war for me and other reporters was trying to work without the help of the U.S. government or without the help of the government in Kuwait. But if you had to rely on the U.S. government, we never would have learned the true story of the war.

—Jack Kelley

[Press coverage of war] is not just a matter of ratings, it's a matter of telling the public how their tax dollars are being spent and what's being done in their name.

—Jane Kirtley

Engaging the press while engaging the enemy is taking on one adversary too many.

—Lt. Col. James Kevin Lovejoy

Television brought the brutality of war into the comfort of the living room. Vietnam was lost in the living rooms of America— not on the battlefields of Vietnam.

—Marshall McLuhan

We spend all day broadcasting on the radio and TV telling people back home what's happening here. And we learn about what's happening here by spending all day monitoring the radio and TV broadcasts from back home.

—P. J. O'Rourke, during the Gulf War

I think American journalists are most patriotic when they retain their skepticism. That isn't cynicism. But we need to think about whether the public needs a flag-waving journalist who says "I'm here because I'm mostly an American and not a journalist" or whether they need good, reliable, solid information . . .

—Geneva Overholser

We don't want the truth told about things here. . . . We don't want the enemy any better informed than he is.

—William Sherman

As I sit tonight . . . the dead and wounded are all around. The knife of the surgeon is busy at work, and amputated legs and arms lies scattered in every direction. The cries of the suffering victim, and the groans of those who patiently await for medical attendance, are most distressing to anyone who has any sympathy with his fellow man. All day long they are coming in. . . . I hope my eyes may never again look upon such sights.

—Ned Spencer, reporting on the
Battle of Shiloh in the Civil War

We were just leeches, reporters trying to suck headlines out of all this death and suffering.

—Robert St. John, World War II correspondent

When Pentagon planners allowed reporters to be "embedded" in the military units that invaded Iraq early in 2003, they took a giant step away from the press-wary policies of the post-Vietnam era. The new policy is promising. But it makes enormous demands on the press and military alike. "Embedded" reporters . . . must resist the temptation to identify too closely with their soldier hosts—to become cheerleaders. And the brass must stick to the policy even when soldiers in the field tell reporters hard truths that deviate from the Pentagon's official line.

—James Tobin

Whereas businessmen and politicians try to enlist journalists for their own purposes, the military man tries to avoid them, and when he cannot, he faces the prospect defensively with a mixture of fear, dread and contempt.

—*Bernard Trainor*

See also *Reporting*

Writers and Writing

A manuscript, like a fetus, is never improved by showing it to somebody before it is completed.

—Anonymous

After being turned down by numerous publishers, he had decided to write for posterity.

—George Ade

He that will write well in any tongue must follow this counsel of Aristotle: to speak as the common people do, to think as wise men do.

—Roger Ascham

Reading maketh the full man, conference a ready man, and writing an exact man.

—Francis Bacon

It's very easy, after all, not to be a writer. Most people aren't writers and very little harm comes to them.

—Julian Barnes

It took me fifteen years to discover I had no talent for writing, but I couldn't give it up because by that time I was too famous.

—Robert Benchley

The pen is mightier than the sword.

—E. G. Bulwer-Lytton

That's not writing, that's typing.
 —*Truman Capote, referring to the work of Jack Kerouac*

The composing room has an unlimited supply of periods available to terminate short, simple sentences.
—*Turner Catledge*

A quotation, like a pun, should come unsought, and then be welcomed only for some propriety or felicity justifying the intrusion.
—*Robert W. Chapman*

Dear God: I like the Lord's Prayer best of all. Did you have to write it a lot or did you get it right the first time? I have to write everything I ever write over again.
—Children's Letters to God

Learn to handle a writing brush and you'll never handle a begging bowl.
—*Chinese proverb*

Writing a book is an adventure: it begins as an amusement, then it becomes a mistress, then a master, and finally a tyrant.
—*Winston Churchill*

A writer can develop only as rapidly as he learns to recognize what is bad in his writing.
—*John Ciardi*

That writer does the most who gives his reader the *most* knowledge and takes from him the *least* time.
—*C. C. Colton*

Better to write for yourself and have no public, than to write for the public and have no self.
—*Cyril Connolly*

In America only the successful writer is important, in France all writers are important, in England no writer is important, and in Australia you have to explain what a writer is.

—Geoffrey Cottrell

Writing is a trade . . . which is learned by writing.

—Simone de Beavoir

The pen is the tongue of the mind.

—Miguel de Cervantes

An original writer is not one who imitates no one, but whom no one can imitate.

—François-René de Chateaubriand

The Lord created heaven and earth and, as an immediate after-thought, writers.

—Fred de Cordova

Wherever citizens are seen routinely as enemies of their own government, writers are routinely seen to be the most dangerous enemies.

—E. L. Doctorow

Writing is like driving a car at night. You can only see as far as the headlights, but you make the whole trip that way.

—E.L. Doctorow

Only the hand that erases can write the true thing.

—Meister Eckhart

Blessed is the man who, having nothing to say, abstains from giving in words evidence of the fact.

—George Eliot

Cats gotta scratch. Dogs gotta bite. I gotta write.

—James Elroy

People do not deserve to have good writing, they are so pleased with bad.

—Ralph Waldo Emerson

If you wish to be a writer, write.

—Epictetus

Be careful that you write accurately rather than much.

—Erasmus

The tools I need for my work are paper, tobacco, food and a little whiskey.

—William Faulkner

You never stop a running horse to give him sugar.

—William Faulkner, on why one should never praise working writers

No tears in the writer, no tears in the reader. No surprise for the writer, no surprise for the reader.

—Robert Frost

He who does not expect a million readers should not write a line.

—Johann Wolfgang von Goethe

Though you may write with an angel's pen yet your work will have no mercantile value unless you are known as an author. Emerson would be twice as well known if he had written for the magazines a little just to let common people know of his existence.

—Horace Greeley, writing to Henry David Thoreau

Nothing you write will ever come out as you first hoped.

—Lillian Hellman

Easy writing makes hard reading.

—*Ernest Hemingway*

The most essential gift for a good writer is a built-in shock-proof shit detector.

—*Ernest Hemingway*

We are all apprentices in a craft where no one becomes a master.

—*Ernest Hemingway*

Write what you like; there is no other rule.

—*O. Henry*

You will have written exceptionally well if, by skillful arrangement of your words, you have made an ordinary one seem original.

—*Horace*

Now if you can write out of the sense that you're going to die as soon as the work is done, then you will write with urgency, honesty, courage and without flinching at all, as if this were the last testament in language, the last utterance you could ever make to anybody. If a work is written like that, then I want to read it.

—*Derrick Jensen*

The greatest part of a writer's time is spent in reading.

—*Samuel Johnson*

Your manuscript is both good and original, but the part that is good is not original and the part that is original is not good.

—*Samuel Johnson*

The incurable itch of writing possesses many.

—*Juvenal*

All of us learn to write in the second grade. Most of us go on to greater things.

> —*Bobby Knight, basketball coach*

A writer's ambition should be . . . to trade a hundred contemporary readers for ten readers in ten years time and for one reader in a hundred years.

> —*Arthur Koestler*

The way to write is well, and how is your own business.

> —*A. J. Liebling*

Every journalist has a novel in him, which is an excellent place for it.

> —*Russell Lynes*

He writes nothing whose writings are not read.

> —*Martial*

Only a mediocre writer is always at his best.

> —*W. Somerset Maugham*

To write simply is as difficult as to be good.

> —*W. Somerset Maugham*

The point of good writing is knowing when to stop.

> —*Lucy M. Montgomery*

I always do the first line well, but I have trouble with the others.

> —*Molière*

The one thing that comforts me most as I pass through terminal middle age is that I shall never learn to write. I can always try new forms, new subjects, new voices. Each day at my desk I will find new and interesting ways to fail.

> —*Don Murray*

The role of the writer is not to say what we can all say, but what we are unable to say.

—Anaïs Nin

The writer who loses sight of his reader is not really writing at all; he is merely making marks on paper.

—Gene Olson

Everywhere I go I'm asked if I think the university stifles writers. My opinion is that they don't stifle enough of them. There's many a bestseller that could have been prevented by a good teacher.

—Flannery O'Connor

Everything that is written merely to please the author is worthless.

—Blaise Pascal

Put it to them briefly so that they will read it, clearly so they will appreciate it, picturesquely so they will remember it, and, above all, accurately, so they will be guided by its light.

—Joseph Pulitzer

Men should use common words to say uncommon things; but they do the reverse.

—Arthur Schopenhauer

Writers are a little below clowns and a little above trained seals.

—John Steinbeck

Writing is the only thing that, when I do it, I don't feel I should be doing something else.

—Gloria Steinem

A sentence should contain no unnecessary words, a paragraph no unnecessary sentences, for the same reason that a drawing should have no unnecessary lines and a machine no unnecessary parts.

—William Strunk Jr. and E. B. White

Proper words in proper places make the true definition of style.

—Jonathan Swift

Pens are most dangerous tools, more sharp by odds
Than swords, and cut more keen than whips or rods.

—John Taylor

You have to hold your audience in writing to the very end—much more than in talking, when people have to be polite and listen to you.

—Brenda Ueland

If you are killed because you are a writer, that's the maximum expression of respect.

—Mario Vargas Llosa

Blank paper is God's way of telling us that it's not so easy to be God.

—Craig Vettner

God lets you write; he also lets you not write.

—Kurt Vonnegut Jr.

Who is more to be pitied: a writer bound and gagged by policemen or one living in perfect freedom who has nothing more to say?

—Kurt Vonnegut Jr.

Sometimes marvelous rushes of words will just fall into place. Other times you have to put your head in a vise and make them come out.

—*Tom Wolfe*

Credibility is just as fragile for a writer as for a President.

—*William Zinsser*

See also *Language and Words*

Index of names

A

Abrams, Floyd 56
Ace, Goodman 142, 220
Achenbach, Joel 215
Adams, Eddie 152
Adams, John Quincy . . . 100, 170
Ade, George 142, 245
Adler, Mortimer 192
Aeschylus 133
Agnew, Spiro . . . . . xiii, 117, 220
Ahmed, Akbar S. 162
Allen, Fred 220
Allen, Woody 188, 220
Alsop, Joseph 199, 204
Alsop, Stewart 204
Alter, Jonathan 117, 220
Alterman, Eric 56
Altschull, J. Herbert 100
Aylesworth, Merlin H. 188
Amanpour, Christiane 240
American Civil Liberties Union 26
Anderson, Peter 35
Andrews, Peter 240
Anne, Princess 152
Anonymous 3, 11, 26, 35, 39,
    51, 114, 133, 152, 183, 188, 199,
    213, 221, 245
Anthony, Edward 26
Appel, Alfred 117
Arbus, Diane 152
Aristotle 26
Arlen, Michael 221
Arnold, Matthew 90

Ascham, Roger 245
Ascherson, Neal 213
Aspen Daily News 125
Associated Press Managing
    Editors 183
The Atlanta Journals 125
Attlee, Clement 133
Atwood, M. V. 66
Auden, W. H. 49, 100, 117
Auletta, Ken 234
Austen, Jane 133
Ayckbourn, Alan 142

B

Bacon, Francis 174, 245
Bagdikian, Ben H. 56, 80, 117,
    199, 215, 221
Bagehot, Walter 11
Baillie, Hugh 199
Baker, Ray S. 199
Baker, Russell 35, 183, 221
Bakker, Tammy Faye 221
Baldwin, Stanley 162
Balliett, Whitney 43
The Baltimore Sun 125
Balzar, John 240
Barber, Benjamin 118
Barksdale, James L. 84
Barnum, P. T. 142
Barnes, Clive 221
Barnes, Fred 118
Barnes, Julian 245
Barrie, James 174

Barron, Jerome 20
Barry, Dave 20, 51, 84, 142
Barth, Alan 66
Bartholin, Thomas 11
Bartlett, David 62, 84
Barton, Bruce 3
Batten, James K.. 142
Battino, Dave 195
Baudelaire, Charles 3, 143
Beaumarchais, Pierre-Augustin 56
Beavoir, Simone de 247
Beckett, Denis 133
Beckett, Samuel 105
Beecher, Henry Ward. 3, 143
Beerbohm, Max 43
Behan, Brendan 43, 184
Belloc, Hilaire 11
Benchley, Robert 78, 245
Bennett, Alan 66
Bennett, Arnold 56
Bennett, James Gordon Sr. . . . 39,
    133, 143, 170
Bennett, Jesse Lee 11
Benny, Jack. 188
Bent, Silas 134
Bentley, Nicolas 100
Berenson, Bernard 105
Berg, Bob 57
Berkeley, William. 174
Berkson, Seymour 39
Bernays, Edward L. 184
Bernfeld, Jules E. 20
Bernstein, Carl 90, 134, 170
Berston, Hyman Maxwell . . . 184
The Bettendorf News 125
Bevan, Aneurin 143
Biafra, Jello 195
The Bible 134
Biesecker, Barbara 118
Bird, Robert S. 143
Bird, S. Elizabeth 213
Bird, Rose. 170

Birt, John 157, 234
Bismarck, Otto Von 104
Black, Conrad. 143
Black, Creed. 3
Black, Hugo 4, 62, 80
Blackmun, Harry A.. 27
Blackstone, William. 66
Blakeslee, Alton. 134
Blanchard, Al 39
Boccardi, Louis D. 39, 215
Bogart, Humphrey 162
Bogart, John B 134
Bogart, Leo. 84, 143, 221
Boliska, Al 222
Bolt, Robert 127
Boorstin, Daniel J. 4, 11, 184, 222
Borah, William E. 67
Borges, Jorge Luis 11
Börne, Ludwig 27
Borovoy, A. Alan. 27
Bowdler, Thomas. 27
Bradbury, Ray 222
Bradlee, Benjamin 39, 80
Brady, Mathew 152
Braestrup, Peter 241
Brain, Lord. 222
Brandeis, Louis. 67, 184
Brassaï 152
Brennan, William. 110
Brewer, David 67
Briggs, Charles. 215
Briggs, Jack 57
Brin, David. 204
Brinkley, David 57, 134, 157, 234
Brisbane, Arthur. 49
British Board of Film Censors . 27
British Ministry of
    Information. 177
Britt, Steuart Henderson. 4
Brokaw, Tom 90, 234
Bromfield, Kenneth 4
Brooks, Gwendolyn 57

Brooks, Mel 127
Brossard, Nicole. 105
Broun, Heywood 27, 67
Brown, Craig 35, 90
Brown, H. Jackson 134, 204
Brown, Himan 18
Brown, John Mason 222, 233
Brown, Les. 222
Brown, Willie. 204
Bryson, Bill 222
Buchwald, Art 157, 222
Buffet, Warren 20, 101
Bulwer-Lytton, E. G. . . . 181, 245
Buñuel, Luis. 127
Burger, Warren E.. 110
Burgess, Anthony. 43
Burgin, David. 134
Burson, Harold. 185
Bush, Barbara. 165
Bush, Vannevar 215
Butler, Samuel 39, 105

C
Caen, Herb 36
Caine, Michael. 127
Califano, Joseph A. Jr.. 204
Calisher, Hortense 105
Cameron, James. 40
Campbell, Don. 185
Campbell, Patrick. 90
Camus, Albert 67
Canby, Vincent. 127
Cannon, Jimmy 211
Canrey, Jim. 40
Capote, Truman246
Capra, Frank. 127
Carey, James. 90
Carlile, Richard 174
Carlyle, Thomas. . . . 12, 144, 174
Carroll, Lewis. 12, 105, 106
Carson, Johnny. 222
Carter, Hodding 101, 205

Carter, Jimmy. 165
Casson, Hugh. 223
Cater, Douglass 134
Catledge, Turner. 80, 246
Cavett, Dick 223
Cervantes, Miguel de 247
Chafee, Zechariah Jr. 67, 162, 170
Chaffee, Edmund B. 67
Chancellor, John. 118
Chandler, Raymond 52
Channing, William Ellery 12
Chaplin, Charlie. 128
Chapman, Robert W. 246
Charles, Roger 200
Chase, Stuart 4
Chateaubriand, François-René de
    247
Chayefsky, Paddy. 46, 223
Chekhov, Anton. 91
Chesterfield, Lord. 106
Chesterton, G. K. . . . 91, 135, 188
Children's Letters to God. . . . 246
Childs, Marquis W.. . . . . . 91, 135
Chinese proverb 12, 106, 246
Chomsky, Noam. 85, 118
Chung, Connie 234
Churchill, Winston 106, 170,
    205, 241, 246
Ciardi, John 49, 246
Clark, Roy Peter. 205
Clarke, Arthur C.162
Clinton, Bill 165
Cloud, Stan. 200
Clurman, Richard. 215
Cobb, Irvin S. 36
Cockburn, Alexander. 91
Cockburn, Claud 57
Cocteau, Jean 128
Cohen, Bernard 135, 162
Cohen, Jeff. 27
Cohen, Ronald I. 68
Colby, Frank Moore 101

Cole, Peter 85
Colton, C. C. 68, 246
Commager, Henry Steele 68
Commission on Freedom
    of the Press 57, 119
Cone, Fairfax 4
Confucius 106
Connolly, Cyril 12, 91, 246
Connolly, William G. 144
Conti, Tom 128
Constant, Benjamin 144
Cook, Mark 27
Cooke, Alistair 62, 200
Cooper, Gary 128
Cooper, James Fenimore 163, 170
Cooper, Kent 153
Coren, Alan 223
Corkery, P. J. 214
Cottrell, Geoffrey 247
Coughlin, Laurence C. 223
Cowles, John 20, 144
Cowper, William 171
Creamer, Anita 205
Crichton, Michael 119
Cronin, Mary J. 85
Cronkite, Walter 46, 85, 157,
    158, 235
Crosby, John 144
Cuadra, Pablo Antonio 28
Cuomo, Mario 63
Cuppy, Will 175
Curley, John 200
Curran, Charles 36
Cynic's Cyclopaedia 114

D

Daily Herald 125
Daley, Richard J. 205
Dalzell, Stewart R. 85
D'Amato, Alfonse 158
Dana, Charles 91, 134, 135
Daniel, Samuel 12
Daniels, Draper 4

Daniels, Josephus 28
d'Arcy, Jean 119
Davenport, Walter 52
Davis, Clive 195
Day, Robin 223
Deakin, Ralph 135
Deaver, Michael 205
de Cordova, Fred 247
De Forest, Lee 223, 224
DeMille, Cecil B. 128, 185
Debs, Eugene 63
Dees, Morris 63
Demarest, David 40
Dennis, Everette E. 81
Deneuve, Catherine 153
Descartes, René 12
DeVore, Jack 171
Diamond, Edwin 224
Diana, Princess 153, 205
Dickens, Charles 92
Diogenes 68
Disney, Walt 128
Disraeli, Benjamin 106
Ditka, Mike 211
Dixit, Kunda 85
Doctorow, E. L. 247
Dodd, Andy 195
Dole, Robert 128, 158
Dos Passos, John 188
Douglas, Kirk 28,
Douglas, Mike 158
Douglas, Norman 5
Douglas, William O. . . 28, 68, 69,
    110
Downie, Leonard Jr. 46
Dreiser, Theodore 21
Drucker, Peter 5, 49
Drudge, Matt 86
"Dub" 196
Duhamel, Georges 128
Dunne, Finley Peter . 52, 144, 163
Duras, Marguerite 58
Dworkin, Ronald 69

E

Eagan, J. W. 12
Easterbrook, Frank Hoover . . . 69
Eastwood, Clint 128
Eban, Abba. 177
Eckhart, Meister. 247
The Economist 86, 135
Edelman, Maurice 28
Edwards, Tryon 40
Ehrenreich, Barbara 69
Ehrlich, Dan 69
Eisenhower, Dwight D. . . 28, 165, 241
Eisner, Michael 21
Eliot, George 247
Eliot, T. S. 52, 119, 224
Elliott, Osborn 235
Elroy, James 247
Emerson, Gloria 241
Emerson, Ralph Waldo . . . 28, 46, 192, 248
English proverb 12, 135
Ephron, Nora 235
Epictetus. 248
Epstein, Edward Jay. 205
Erasmus 13, 246
Erickson, A. J. 153
Erskine, Thomas. 81
Erskine, John 181
Estrich, Susan. 171
Evans, Harold. 153
Evening Standard (London). . . . 5
Exley, Helen 13

F

Faber, Harold 206
Fanning, Shaun. 196
Farnsworth, Philo T. 224
Faulkner, William 248
Feather, William. 5
Ferrari, Doug 224
Femina, Jerry Della 5
Fenwick, Millicent 63

Fielding, Henry 145
Fitzgerald, F. Scott. 5, 106
Fitzgerald, Zelda 6
Flanagan, Hallie 189
Foot, Michael 145
Foreman, Gene. 206
Forman, Milos 28
Fowler, Gene 52
France, Anatole 13
Frank, Barney. 81
Frank, Florence Kipper 13
Frank, Glenn. 6
Frank, Jerome D. 177
Frank, Reuven 136, 171, 235
Frankfurter, Felix 69, 111
Franklin, Benjamin 29, 52, 70, 145
Frazier, George. 129
Frederick the Great. 70
Freud, Sigmund 29
Friend, David 153
Friendly, Fred 200, 224, 236
Friedman, Thomas L. 136
Frohnmayer, John. 63, 224
Frost, David 224
Frost, Robert. 248
Fry, Christopher 43
Fuller, Jack. 58
Fuller, Thomas 106
Fuller, R. Buckminster. 224
Funkhouser, G. Ray 81

G

Gabler, Neal 136
Gaines, Jim. 119
Galbraith, John Kenneth . . 6, 158
Gallup, George. 192
Garbett, Cyril 43
Gandhi, Indira 29
Gandhi, Mahatma. 70
Gartner, Michael 70, 92, 206
Gates, Bill. 86, 87, 175
Gates, Henry Louis Jr. 29

Gédalge, Andre 43
Geisel, Theodore
  ("Dr. Seuss") 106
Gergen, David 185
Gernsheim, Helmut 154
Gershwin, George 196
Ghiglione, Loren 101
Gibbs, Wolcott 114
Gilder, George 87
Giles, William E. 136
Gillmor, Don 111
Gillon, Philip 136
Gingrich, Newt. 158
Ginsberg, Allen 119
Giradoux, Jean 163
Gitlin, Todd 6, 21, 120, 216
Gleason, Jackie. 44
Godard, Jean-Luc. 129
Godfrey, Mark 154
Godwin, Mike 87
Goebbels, Joseph 177, 189
Goethe, Johann von 248
Goldberg, Bernard 40
Goldschmidt, Neil 49
Goldwater, Barry 163
Goldwyn, Sam 129, 225
Gompers, Samuel. 70
Goodman, Ellen 36
Goodwin, Richard N. 136
Gordon, Karen Elizabeth 107
Gordon, Matt Wells 236
Göring, Hermann 178
Gossage, Howard L. 6
Gordimer, Nadine. 29
Gould, Glenn 196
Grace, Princess. 206
Gracian, Baltasar 137
Graff, Henry. 171
Graham, Philip L. 92
Gramm, Phil. 158
Granger, Bill. 58
Grass, Günter 13

Graves, Robert 78
Gray, Charles 158
Greeley, Horace 248
Green, Robert. 70
Greenberg, Daniel S. 137
Greene, Bob 36
Greene, Graham. 92
Greener, Bill. 145
Greenfeld, Jeff 63
Griffith, Thomas. 53, 92
Griffith-Jones, Mervyn. 29
Griswold, A. Whitney 29, 44
Grossman, Lawrence K. 21
Gump, Forrest 145
The Guardian. 87
Gunther, John. 92
Gutiérrez, Felix F. 192

H

Haagensen, Kenneth. 185
Hadas, Moses 13
Hagerty, James C.. 36
Halberstam, David 70
Haldane, J. B. S. 30
Hamilton, Alexander 71
Hampton, Christopher 44
Hand, Learned 63, 163, 185
Hardwicke, Cedric 225
Harper, Jennifer 120
Harrington, Alan 185
Harrington, John. 13
Hart, Gary 159
Harvard Business Review 6
Harwood, Richard 206
Hayakawa, S. I. 225
Hearst, William Randolph. . . . 58,
  145, 241
Hecht, Ben 58, 145
Heckman, Carey. 87
Heine, Heinrich 28
Hellman, Lillian 248
Helps, Arthur 13

Helvétius, Claude-Adrien. 30
Hemingway, Ernest . 36, 146, 249
Henry, O. 249
Henry, William A. III. 46
Hepburn, Katherine 185
Hersey, John 58, 92
Hess, John Loft 137
Hesse, Herman 107
Hewitt, Don 40, 236
Heyward, Andrew 236
Hitchcock, Alfred. 129
Higgins, Michael D. 145
Hilliard, Robert 189
Hine, Lewis 154
Hitler, Adolf. 30, 178
Hocking, Willliam Ernest 21
Hockney, David 154
Hoffman, Abbie 107
Hoffman, Dustin. 44
Hogg, Michael 58
Holmes, Oliver Wendell Jr. 13, 71
Holmes, Oliver Wendell Sr. 44, 71
Hoover, Herbert . . . 165, 166, 189
Horace 249
Howard, Phillip 18
Howe, E. W. 200
Hubbard, Elbert 53, 175
Hughes, Charles Evans 171
Hulme, Thomas Ernest. 107
Hume, Ellen 92
Humphrey, Hubert H. 71
Humphreys, John 137
Huneker, James Gibbons 44
Husni, Samir. 114
Hutchins, Robert Maynard . . 207, 225
Huxley, Aldous . . . 7, 30, 40, 107, 178

I

Ickes, Harold L. 37
ibn-Tibbon, Judah 14

Ingrams, Richard 111
Inter-American Press
  Association 201
Irani, Cushrow R. 71
Irving, John 146
Italian proverb 14, 137
Ito, Lance 58, 111

J

Jabotinsky, Vladimir. 107
Jackson, Jesse. 120
Jackson, Joseph Henry. 30
The Jacksonville Daily News . 125
Jacobi, Ernst. 53
Jacobsen, Hugh Newell 37
Jacobson, Sidney 159
Jaffe, Erwin 216
Jagger, Mick. 37
James, Clive 129, 225
Jamieson, Kathleen Hall . . 41, 93, 159
Jaspin, Elliot. 216
Jayaweera, Neville 120
Jefferson, Thomas 7, 71, 111, 146, 159, 171
Jennings, Peter 93
Jensen, Derrick. 53, 249
Jewish proverb 14
John Paul II, Pope 120
Johnson, Haynes. 159
Johnson, Hiram 242
Johnson, Lyndon B. 46, 166
Johnson, Nicholas . . 21, 120, 225
Johnson, Paul 21
Johnson, Samuel . . . 7, 31, 53, 78, 101, 242, 249
Johnson, W. Thomas. 236
Jones, Jenkin Lloyd 225
Joubert, Joseph 107, 192
Journalist's Creed. 93
Journalists' slogan 64
Jovanovich, William. . . . 107, 192

Juvenal 249
Jung, Carl 129

K

Kael, Pauline 129, 130, 179
Kafka, Franz 14
Kaltenborn, H. V 137
Kalven, Harry Jr. 111
Katoppo, Aristides 120
Katz, Jon 111, 146
Kavanagh, Patrick 146
Keaton, Michael 130
Keillor, Garrison 189
Kelen, Emery 53
Kelly, Kevin 196, 197
Kelley, Jack 242
Kelmenson, Leo-Arthur 7
Kelvin, Lord 189
Kempis, Thomas à 14
Kennedy, Jacqueline 166
Kennedy, John F. . . . 81, 166, 181
Kent, Frank 159
Kerby, Philip 64
Kerner Commission on Civil
    Disorders 121
Ketter, William B. 147
Khrushchev, Nikita S. . . 171, 226
Kierkegaard, Sören . . 72, 81, 101,
    226
Kilpatrick, James J. 54,
Kindred, Dave 93
King, Colbert 59
King, Henry 93
Kipling, Rudyard 108, 201
Kirby, Robert 7, 31
Kirtley, Jane 82, 111, 242
Kitman, Marvin 226
Klein, Jeffrey 121
Knickerbocker, H. R. 102
Knight, Bobby 250
Knightley, Phillip 83
Knoll, Erwin 59
Koestler, Arthur 250

Kohl, Louise 54
Konner, Joan 94
Koppel, Ted 37, 72, 201, 216
Kovach, Bill 94
Kozinski, Alex 72
Kraus, Karl 102, 163, 171
Kristol, William 115
Kronenberg, Frank J. 226
Kronenberger, Louis 37
Kume, Hiroshi 237
Kundera, Milan 14
Kuralt, Charles 237
Kurtz, Howard 147

L

Lambert, Constant 197
Landers, Ann 226
Landor, Walter Savage 108
Lange, Dorothea 154
Lapham, Lewis H. 94
Laski, Harold J. 22, 137
Lassalle, Ferdinand 22
Latvian Jewish Community
    Council 14
Lazarsfeld, Paul 163
Leacock, Stephen 7
Lebowitz, Fran 115, 189,
    226
Lec, Stanislaw 147
Ledeen, Michael 159
Lee, Ivy 179
Legal maxim 112
Lenin, Nikolai 72
Leo XIII, Pope 172
Lerner, Max 37
Levant, Oscar 130
Levinson, Leonard Louis 147
Lewis, C. S. 14
Lewis, Joseph 31
Lewis, Sinclair 7, 102
Lewis, Wilmott 192
Lichtenberg, Georg Christoph . . 14
Liddy, G. Gordon 172

Liebling, A. J. .. 47, 72, 102, 137, 172, 201, 250
Lincoln, Abraham .. 72, 181, 182
Lindsay, John 159
Lindstrom, Carl E. 54
Linedecker, Cliff 214
Lippmann, Walter 59, 72, 73, 82, 94, 102, 137, 164, 166, 179, 186, 216
Little, Lou. 211
Loevinger, Lee 137, 226, 227
Longfellow, Henry Wadsworth 44
Long-Scott, Austin. 59
Lopez, Jennifer. 154
Lott, Trent 160
Lovejoy, James Kevin . . . . . : 242
Luce, Henry R. 59, 102, 115
Lueck, Therese. 115
Lumière, August 130
Luther, Martin 15
Lynd, Robert 138
Lynes, Russell 250

M

MacEwen, Arthur. 138
Machiavelli. 179
MacNeil, Robert. . 47, 94, 95, 237
MacNeil, Robin 214
MacNelly, Jeff 59
Macaulay, Rose 147
Macaulay, Thomas 172
Madison, James 47, 172
Madonna. 73
Maher, Bill. 227
Mailer, Norman 41, 227
Malay proverb 108
Malcolm, Derek 211
Malcolm, Janet. 60
Malcolm X 164
Malraux, André 82
Mancroft, Lord. 22
Mandela, Nelson. 47, 160
Mankiewicz, Frank. 237

Mann, Judy. 54
The Marble Hill Era. 125
Marcuse, Herbert 121
Margach, James 160
Márquez, Gabriel García 95
Marsh, Daniel. 227
Markel, Lester 121
Martial 31, 250
Martineau, Harriet 193
Martz, Larry. 31
Marven, Lee. 41
Marx, Groucho. 227
Marx, Karl 78
Marzolf, Marion Tuttle. 22
Mashek, John 201
Mason, George. 73
Mason, Nick. 197
Maugham, W. Somerset .. 44, 250
Maverick, Augustus. 215
May, Rollo 108
Maynard, Nancy Hicks . 103, 121
McCarthy, Eugene J. 201
McCaskill, Ian 237
McChesney, Robert 88
McCormick, Robert 147
McEnroe, John. 211
McGinniss, Joe. 160
McGuff, Joe 211
McLuhan, Marshall. . 8, 121, 216, 217, 227, 242
McMasters, Paul. 31
Mead, Margaret 227
Mears, Walter. 82
Megary, A. Roy 22
Meiklejohn, Alexander 73
Mekas, Jonas 130
Mencken, H. L. . 54, 95, 121, 147
Menuhin, Yehudi 147
Merrill, Mary Lee. 121
Merritt, Davis "Buzz" 48, 95
Merton, Robert. 163
Metcalfe, Robert. 217
Meyer, Alan H. 7

Meyer, Phillip. 95
Meyerowitz, Joshua 227
Michener, James. 167
Mill, James. 73
Mill, John Stuart. 31, 73
Millay, Edna St. Vincent 15
Miller, Arthur. 148
Miller, Frank Jr. 96
Miller, Jonathan 32
Miller, Mark C. 227
Miller, Paul. 8
Milne, A. A. 108
Milton, John 32, 73
Minow, Newton 228, 230
Mizner, Wilson. 44
Molière. 250
Montaigne 108
Montesquieu. 198
Montgomery, Lucy M. 250
Morgan, Edward P. 15
Morgan, Thomas 207
Morley, Christopher 15
Morris, William S. III 217
Morrison, Van. 197
Morse, Samuel 218
Mortimer, John. 32
Morton, J. B. 54
Mougayar, Walid 88
Moyers, Bill 103, 228
Moynihan, Daniel P. 74
Muggeridge, Malcolm . . . 96, 229
Murdoch, Rupert 193
Murphy, Frank 22
Murray, Don 202, 250
Murray, John. 15
Murrow, Edward R. . 22, 189, 229
Muskie, Edmund S. 207

N

Nachman of Bratslav 15
Napoleon 82, 103, 138
Nash, Ogden. 8

National Commission on Causes
  and Prevention of Violence 230
Nauman, Art. 60
Nehru, Jawaharlal. 74
Naisbett, John. 121
The National Enquirer 126
Nessen, Ron 207, 230, 238
Neuborne, Burt. 74
Neuharth, Al. 103, 122, 193
Newman, Paul 112, 154
The New York Sun 126
The New York Times 94, 118,
  126, 137, 144, 148
New Yorker cartoon . . . 8, 88, 116
Newsroom adage 103
Newton, John 148, 167
Nietzsche, Friedrich 41, 179
Nin, Anaïs 251
Nixon, Richard M. 47, 160,
  167, 168, 230
Norden, Dennis 230
Northcliffe, Lord 96, 122,
  138, 193
Northwest Conference
  of the Methodist Episcopal
  Church 148

O

Oakes, John 47
O'Brien, Conan 230
O'Brien, Emmet N. 103
O'Brien, Flann 108
Ochs, Adolph S. 148
O'Connor, Flannery 251
O'Connor, John J. 231
Ogilvy, David 3, 8
Olson, Gene 251
O'Neill, Mike. 48
O'Rourke, P. J. 60, 242
Orwell, George. 8, 41, 179
Outing magazine 155
Overholser, Geneva 207, 243

Owen, Ken 32
Ozick, Cynthia 108

P

Page, Arthur W. 186
Paley, William S. . . . 18, 122, 238
Pankhurst, Christabel 161
Parris, Matthew 231
Pascal, Blaise 251
Patterson, Eugene 193
Pearl, Mike 214
Pearl, Steven 231
Pearson, Drew 202
Pedro II 218
Peres, Shimon 48
Perlman, S. J. 79
Perry, James 202
Peter, Laurence 231
Peters, Charles 202
Peterson, Theodore 103
Pfizer, Beryl 138
Phillips, Wendell 175
Picard, Max 190
Pickford, Mary 130
Pilkington Report 231
Pimlott, J. A. R. 186
Pitsuwan, Surin 172
Pippert, Wes 60
Pitney, Mahlon 138
Pitt, William 172
Plato 32
Plautus 41
Poe, Edgar Allen 115
Pollock, Channing 44
Pool, Ithiel de Sola 218
Poorman, Paul 64
Pope, Alexander 175
Postman, Neil 218
Potter, Stephen 45
Pound, Ezra 138
Povich, Elaine 161
Powell, Adam Clayton III 23

Powell, Enoch 161
Powell, Jody 138, 167
Powell, Lewis Jr. 64
Power, Jonathan 148
Powers, Ron 238
Powers, William 139
Preston, Keith 115
Prichard, Peter S. 207
Priestland, Gerald 104, 122,
193, 202
Priestley, J. B. 193
Preuss, Joaquim 116
Project for Excellence
in Journalism 122, 139
Prothrow-Stith, Deborah 74
Public Relations Society of
America 186
Pulitzer, Joseph 23, 41, 55,
82, 96, 122, 148, 251
Puttnam, David 131

Q

Quayle, Marilyn 207
Quinn, Jane Bryant 96
Quintillian 108
Quittner, Joshua 88

R

Radio Act of 1927 18
Ramaphosa, Cyril 48
Randall, David 60
Randolph, Eleanor 123
Rapping, Elayne 139
Rascoe, Burton 96
Raskin, Abe 172
Raspberry, William 64, 123
Rather, Dan 97, 207, 238
Rauch, William 202
Raymer, Steve 155
Reagan, Ronald . . . 131, 155, 164,
168, 169
Rehnquist, William 64

Reeves, Rosser 8
Reisman, David 109
Remnick, David 97
Reno, Janet 231
Reston, James . . 37, 139, 168, 200
Reuss, Carol 123
Rich, Frank 23
Rice, Grantland 211
Richelieu, Cardinal 32
Richards, Kelli 195
Richter, Jean Paul 109
Riis, Jacob 155
Rivers, William 208
Roberts, Gene 97
Robinson, Kinsey M. 186
Rogers, Joel Augustus 179
Rogers, Will 103, 148
Rogers, Warren 208
Roosevelt, Eleanor 9
Roosevelt, Franklin D. . 9, 33, 182
Roosevelt, Theodore 74, 82
Rosen, Jay 48, 97
Rosenblatt, Roger 139
Rosenblum, Mort 139
Ross, Harold 55, 116
Rosten, Leo 104
Rousseau, Jean Jacques 33
Rowan, Carl 202
Royster, Vermont 74
Rundgren, Todd 197
Runnion, Norman 50
Rushdie, Salmon 75, 140
Ruskin, John 15
Russell, Bertrand . . . 75, 179, 182
Russell, Foster Meharny 41
Rutledge, John 112
Ryan, William 33

S

Safire, William 37, 94
Saguisag, Rene 123
Saki 41
Saltzberg, Barney 109

Sanborn, F. B. 148
Sanford, Bruce W. 60, 208
Santayana, George 9
Sarnoff, David 60, 190
Sarraute, Nathalie 19
Sass, Gerald M. 104
Scalia, Antonin 65
Scannell, Don 212
Scargill, Arthur 208
Schell, Jonathan 161
Scheer, Robert 33, 209
Schmertz, Herb 186
Schmidt, Helmut 48
Schopenhauer, Arthur . . . 15, 148,
    251
Schorr, Daniel 123, 161
Schudson, Michael 164
Schumach, Murray 231
Schumaker, Thomas 112
Scott, C. P. 23, 42, 232
Scribner, Charles 16
Scheer, Robert 33, 209
Seinfeld, Jerry 148, 232
Scripps, E. W. 173
The Scripps Howard Newspaper
    Group 126
Seib, Charles 140
Seinfeld, Jerry 148, 232
Serling, Rod 232
Sevareid, Eric 23, 238
Shalit, Gene 131
Shakespeare, William . . . 88, 112,
    140, 202
Shaw, George Bernard . . . 33, 45,
    97, 149
Shelley, James 19
Shephard, Sam 131
Sheridan, Richard Brinsley . . 149
Sherman, William 243
Sibelius, Jean 45
Siegel, Ed 97
Sigal, Leon 140
Silensky, Robert 88

Simon, Paul 202
Simone, Nina 197
Simpson, Alan K. 82
Simpson, O. J. 58, 111, 209
Sloan, Bill 214
Smallwood, Lois 75
Smith, Anthony 38, 123, 218
Smith, Margaret Chase. 75
Smith, Merriman 168
Smith, R. C. 116
Smith, Wallace 203
Smith, "Wolfman Jack" 190
Smyser, Dick 149
Snead, Sam. 212
Sneed, Joseph P. 75
Snow, Tony 218
Snyder, Tom. 190
Society of Professional
    Journalists. 61
Solzhenitsyn, Alexander. . 83, 173
Sontag, Susan. 155
Spanish proverb 149
Speakes, Larry 168
Spence, Gerry. 232
Spencer, Earl 209
Spencer, Ned 243
Spender, Stephen 173
Springer, Jerry 239
St. John, Robert 243
Stalin, Joseph 131, 175
Stallone, Sylvester 131
Stead, W. Jr. 149
Steele, Robert M. 97
Steichen, Edward 156
Stein, Gertrude 123
Stein, Joel 113
Stein, Robert. 124
Steinbeck, John 16, 251
Steinem, Gloria 251
Stern, Howard 232
Stereo Review. 198
Stevens, John Paul 113
Stevenson, Adlai 42, 53, 75

Stevenson, Robert Louis 16
Stewart, Potter 33, 65
Stolley, Richard B. 116
Stone, I. F. 23
Stoppard, Tom 124, 149, 203
Storey, Wilbur F. 140, 149
Stroustrup, Bjarne 218
Strachey, Evelyn John 23
Streisand, Barbra 187
Stross, Randall 198
Strout, Richard 173
Strunk, William Jr. 252
Struthers, Sally. 33
Sullivan, Arthur 198
Sulzburger, Arthur Hays 182, 194
Sussman, Leonard R. 75
Sutherland, George. 75
Swaffer, Hannen. 24
Sweeney, Kevin 140
Swift, Jonathan. 252
Swope, Herbert Bayard 42
Sylvester, Arthur D. 180
Syrus, Publilius 76, 140

T

Taft, William H. 168
Taylor, John 252
Tanner, Jack 55
Tauke, Tom. 65
Teresa, Mother 209
Thiers, Louis Adolphe 83
Thomas, Caitlin 209
Thompson, Robert 219
Thomson, Lord. 24, 149
Thoreau, Henry David 140,
    150, 219, 248
Thurm, Samuel. 9
Thurow, Lester 219
Tobin, James. 243
Tolstoy, Leo 16, 98, 175
Tomalin, Nicolas 98, 141
Tomlin, Lily 232
Tocqueville, Alexis de 57, 68

Trainor, Bernard 244
Trento, Susan 187
Trotsky, Leon 190
Truman, Harry S. 83, 168, 169
Tse-Tung Mao 16
Tuchman, Barbara 16
Tucker, Laurie 88
Tunstall, Jeremy 9
Tupper, Martin 16
Turner, E. S. 9
Turner, Ed. 124
Turner, Ted 24, 162, 239
Twain, Mark 16, 42, 55, 79, 109, 113, 124, 203
Tweed, William Marcy 161
Tynan, Kenneth 33, 45
Tyson, Mike 16

U

Ubell, Earl 187
Ueland, Brenda. 252
United Artists
  casting executive 131
Universal Declaration
  of Human Rights 76
Untermeyer, Louis 79
Updike, John 88
U.S. Constitution 65
Ustinov, Peter. 45

V

Valenti, Jack 131
Valéry, Paul 9, 141
van Brocklin, Norm 212
Van Doren, Charles 232
Van Horne, Harriet. 233
Vanocur, Sander 141
Vargas Llosa, Mario 252
Vaz, Sérgio 150
Vettner, Craig 252
Vidal, Gore 131, 169, 194

Voltaire 17, 34, 42, 76, 141, 180, 182
Vonnegut, Kurt Jr. 252

W

Waldman, Paul 41
Walesa, Lech 76
Walker, Alice 233
Wall Street Journal 24
Wallace, DeWitt 116
Walters, Barbara. 203
Wanamaker, John 10
Ward, Joseph 150
Warhol, Andy 124
Warner, Harry 131
Warren, Earl 34, 212
Warren, Robert Penn 79
Was, Don 198
Waters, Muddy 198
Wattenberg, Ben J. 203
Waugh, Evelyn 141
Weber, Max 104
Weisberger, Bernard A. 83
Weisman, Steven R. 169
Welles, Orson 190, 233
Wellington, Duke of 209
Wells, H. G. 55
Wesley, John. 17
West, Mae. 34
West, Rebecca 34, 98, 141
Westmoreland, William 34
Westin, Av 239
Whipple, E. P. 176
White, E. B. 55, 76, 191, 252
White, Theodore H. 203, 233
White, William Allen 10, 24, 25, 50, 55, 76, 150
Whitworth, William 116
Whorf, Benjamin Lee 109
Wicker, Tom. 98
Wilde, Oscar. 17, 42, 98, 169

Wilder, Billy. 132
Wildmon, Don 34
Will, George. 34
Williams, Francis 150
Williams, Gary. 212
Williams, Mason 233
Wills, Garry 77
Wilson, Edmund. 219
Wilson's Photographic
    Magazine 156
Winchell, Walter. 38
Winfrey, Oprah. 194, 233
Winner, Michael. 132
Winogrand, Garry 156
Winship, Thomas 42
Winter, William 151
Wogan, Terry 19
Wolcot, John. 187
Wolcott, James 89
Wolfe, Humbert 104
Wolfe, Tom. 253
Wolsey, Cardinal 176

Woo, William 98
Wood, James Playsted 116
Woodhull, Nancy J. 194
Woodrum, Robert L.. 210
Woodward, Bob 210
Wooten, Jim 61
Worth, Mary 65
Wright, Frank Lloyd 233

Y
Yates, George 156
Yeats, William Butler. 104
Young, Coleman. 113

Z
Zanuck, Darryl F.. 233
Zappa, Frank 124
Zellar, Ed 25
Zinsser, William. 253
Zsigmond, Vilmosa 132
Zoglin, Richard 99